PLANK OWNER:
The Odyssey and Rede

Written By

Gregory White

ISBN-13: 978-0692092873
ISBN-10: 0692092870

This memoir is the story of a kid who ran away from home to become a sailor.

In Memory of Mary Elizabeth and Frank Clifton

"If we're committed to struggle, then we are committed to life, and we are committed to that which never dies . . . I believe in living. I believe in birth. I believe in the sweat of love and the fire of truth. And I believe that a lost ship, steered by tired, sea sick sailors can still be guided home to port."

– Marilyn Jean Buck

"Of all the preposterous assumptions of humanity over humanity, nothing exceeds most of the criticisms made on the habits of the poor by the well-housed, well-warmed, and well-fed."

- Herman Melville

INTRODUCTION

Volunteering with "Project Liberty Ship" in Baltimore, Maryland, I had an opportunity to offer shipboard orientation to a group of young cadets aboard the SS John W. Brown (a functioning World War II Liberty Ship).

These cadets were from the Baltimore Maritime Industries Academy; a public charter school in Baltimore educating inner-city cadets. This is a school with a maritime theme and curriculum. All were seniors in preparation for graduation.

The cadets were attentive and eager. I spoke with the cadets about way of a ship and the way of a shipboard Engineering Department. The entire experience humbled me in a great way.

Beforehand, I was told that some of these cadets lived in areas of the city that were not very stable.

Having been born to young parents, I knew firsthand the challenges of being raised in an inner-city household that was always struggling. I witnessed the adults around me accepting the low paying jobs, menial labor, and extra hours.

With my parents at work I did not know the discipline of parental supervision. I grew up accustomed to having a need of small materials, the simple things that are often commonplace in the more stable or fortunate sectors of our society.

Life is not fair. Yet I do not consider myself a victim.

Living in a poor community, exposed to a poor education, developing poor self-esteem, nurturing reckless ideas – all these factors have been an undeniable reality in young people making poor choices in their lives.

I was a prime example of a young person who succumbed to the challenges of being a poor kid. The odds of achieving goals were against me. Misbehavior made my life worse.

Whether in the inner-city or a rural area – poor is poor. The struggle is real, and poor choices made are detrimental and with consequences. Too many times young people are apt to make a choice, an irrational choice, that is harmful.

I had to reach far beyond the world around me. I had to search and locate positive forces of guidance and support. I had to knock on countless doors to find a way out. Feelings of being trapped was a reality; many young people know this feeling.

Young people need to have "a way out." An exit door should exist – and this exit door should remain unlocked and unobstructed.

The line of communication that I struck up with the cadets from the Baltimore Maritime Industries Academy was natural and without expectation. They were all eager and sharp. Not unlike young people everywhere.

What I saw in the young faces before me was optimism – and a need for opportunity. Having that first chance can very well negate the need for a "second chance" down the line.

What I hoped for the cadets was that, as they matured and learned responsibility, they would take a road in life that always carried them forward.

And that they not be afraid to "knock on doors" and seek positive guidance from others. Good people will be there. The spirit of humanity treads over obstacles.

Take care to strengthen those positive bonds. Develop rational decisions; selecting the choice that best represents [your] opportunity to fulfill a chosen goal.

Make the most of that first chance.

FOREWORD

From 1975 through 1983 the United States Navy commissioned thirty (30) Spruance-Class Destroyers. These magnificent war ships were built at Litton Ingalls Shipbuilding in Pascagoula, Mississippi. Four (4) of these warships were modified and commissioned as Kidd-Class Destroyers, and eventually sold to Taiwan.

Documented in the "commissioning book" that was given to all Plank Owners (I still have mine), the Spruance-Class destroyer had crew complement of 254 Officers and Enlisted men. This would indicate a total of approximately 7700 sailors were honored as "Plank Owner" aboard these thirty (30) illustrious destroyers.

The USS Moosbrugger DD-980 was one of these vessels; commissioned on 16 December 1978. I was honored as one of the 254 Plank Owner's aboard this man-o-war. With admiration and pride, we called her "the 'Moose" for short.

By all accounts this class of ship was the largest destroyer class in the history of the United States Navy. The size and speed of these "tin cans" made them unique and special.

The 'Moose is long gone. One account is that she was taken to a scrap yard and dismantled into pieces. Another account regarding her fate is that she was sank and became part of a man-made reef somewhere in the Atlantic Ocean on the eastern seaboard.

To date, there is only one (1) true Spruance-Class Destroyer still in existence (that I know of), and she is the USS Paul F. Foster DD-964.

In 2015, while in Port Hueneme, California, I saw her tied at dock. From outside of a locked gate, I sat for an hour or more and looked her over.

I thought about how we, the engineers of M Division, would muster for quarters on the helo-deck. The 5 inch .54 caliber guns had been removed from the Foster, but I remembered them, and I recalled in a brief reverie the blasting roar they could produce. Spruance-Class. The biggest "tin can" of them all. Fast and sleek. There she was in all her glorious presence.

It is ironic, and I am open for discussion or challenge, that of which I welcome, that of the roughly 7700 sailors who are distinguished as "Plank Owner" aboard any Spruance-Class destroyer – I may be the only Plank Owner who is still going to sea as a professional mariner or sailor; military or civilian.

The irony is in the fact that I was a troubled young sailor. Reckless, errant, and making all the mistakes. Sailors and shipmates who know me know how I crawled and struggled from the wayside. I was considered "done" a long time ago.

Yet, I did not give up trying to make amends. I was able to find my way, and to keep pressing on for a chance to redeem myself. The responsibility for redemption remains my own.

Even at this writing, my sea bag is packed and sits close to the front door inside my home. I am ready to go down to a pier anywhere in the world and catch a ship. Going to sea is, truly, the central passion of my life.

Let there be no confusion, let it be clear and transparent, I was not the most well behaved sailor. Not by a long shot.

No awards. No badges. No medals. A single ribbon for pistol expert was all I earned. I possessed little in the way of formal education and skill, and even less when it came to worldliness.

Mixed feelings about myself are a reality that I must live with. Yet every price that was demanded (of me) I found a way to pay or barter to meet that price.

In the summer of 1978, when I put on my United States Navy dress white uniform for the first time – that was my prize.

"There is a category of sailor that may possess, "a relationship with the sea that has a dominating effect on his life . . . the relationship can be described in terms of a lifelong love affair with the sea. Sailors seek, and maybe occasionally find, in this relationship something which never seems accessible to them on land. It is hard to say precisely what it is they seek or experience out at sea, but clearly it is an attraction powerful enough to draw them time and again back to the apparently lonely expanses of the ocean."

–   Derek Wilson, "The Circumnavigators"

WITH EAGER AND CHAFED eleven-year old hands, the four of us, Sonny, Alex, Junior, and myself, pulled and tugged, wrenching free the old fiberglass bathtub liner from a heaping mass of rubbish. We had found the pile of debris and trash stacked high on a vacant lot in suburban Prince George's County.

More than a few blotted stains covered the length of the fiberglass, and there was a small crack in the side of the liner. But it would do. We had discovered something unlike anything else we had found. This was something unique. All at once we began to chatter about what to do next.

We had ourselves a vessel, and there was a small body of stagnant water nearby. It could have been a pond or a lake. It was place where we had skipped stones before, a fair amount of water where we had dared each other to swim across the half-mile distance from one shore to the next.

With fancy and ingenuity, mutual ideas and creativity, we fashioned ourselves a craft sound and buoyant, a vessel worthy, at least in our imaginations, to sail the "Seven Seas."

We dubbed our ship the "Always Invincible," and shouted her aloud named several times. Absorbed in our desire we would ply the trades, likening ourselves to the ways and manner of the Freebooter, the Buccaneer, and the globe-trotting Sea Rover of aged fable and harrowed romance. It was an enterprise that was exciting and flush with expectation.

Hoisting our vessel high and just above our heads, we set off double time, making a bee-line in the direction of the small body of water, that, in our energetic passion for adventure and swerving had newly designated as "Pirate Lake."

We were going to sea!

Crossing the reach of "Pirate Lake" was our goal. Gathering our promise, sprinting forward, barking aloud, our cadence rang life into the words of the old sailor's shanty, "Blow High! Blow Low! And So Say We, Sailing Down The Coast Of The High Barbaree!" Our imaginations ran wild and free.

Corresponding ideas, grand visions of buccaneer mannerisms danced beyond our eyes, and in a rush of voices we foretold how we would wreak havoc and wage mayhem upon the shores of any beach in the wake of our adventure. We were coming and there would be a price to pay.

Again, our cadence rang strong, "Blow High! Blow Low! And So Say We! Sailing Down The Coast Of The High Barbaree!," and with vigor we splashed our makeshift but doughty vessel into the water.

The "Always Invincible" bounced and rolled and yawed in the water. Together, the four of us roared with delight, our words losing distinct clarity in the wind.

And the wind beat and clout against the fiberglass hull of our robust little ship. With energetic voices we bellowed and exhorted in cadence again, "Blow High, Blow Low!" as we peered our young faces against the stiff brace of the wind, "And So Say We! Sailing Down The Coast Of The High Barbaree!." Into the summer of our adolescence we sailed.

Being on the water was fascinating. It was uncanny. I had had found something, by chance really, that had touched me in a way that I cannot readily explain nor detail. I wanted to know more about boats and ships. The idea of sailing across the sea seemed comforting even without detail or a plan.

Accordingly, and with a spell that was in the wind, blowing down gently upon the short swells beneath our vessel, held within the summertime play of these few moments, I knew that I wanted to go sea someday. I wanted to know more about seafaring.

This would be my ticket to the rest of the world. I would leave home. I would travel. Someday I would become a sailor.

As a child growing up in Washington, D.C. it had been my wish to escape. The inner-city areas of the Northwest quadrant of D.C., where I was born into, was a tough world. It was the inner-city at best, and the ghetto at worst.

Bullies and street kids roamed the neighborhoods where I lived. Bullies were always looking for trouble. In grade school the bullies were always black students, like myself, always older, bigger and stronger boys. None of them seemed to care that I, like themselves, was a poor black kid, too.

Horseplay and amusing intimidation were accepted. Playful verbal insults took place all the time, and school yard jostling was common.

But things often got worse fast. The expectation of the "worse" was stressful and overbearing. In this tough world I felt alone and unprotected. I was bullied and harassed with threats a great deal.

I was seven-years old when I was punched in the face with a fist for the first time. It was an angry fist.

Getting hit in the face was a shock. Pain radiated over my face. With eyes narrowed in anger, I tried to fight back, and the beating intensified. Lots of punches struck my head and face. A strong volley of cruel blows knocked me down. I remember my lips being bloody, and I remember being scared.

After that first beating, I was beaten too many times to count. Frequently I went home from school in blood and tears. No matter my cry for help, or my weak effort to fight back, I would get beaten down to the ground on a regular basis.

Surviving the streets as a child was difficult. I learned to avoid certain areas. I discovered escape routes and places where I could run to get away from another beating.

But sometimes there was no outlet. This was especially true at the schools I attended.

At one school, there was Jody Pleasants. Jody was an awkward boy with a big nose. He was tall and strong. Well established as a trouble maker at school, Jody relished attacking smaller kids.

Occasionally, he would fly into a rage and take a swing at an adult. Jody was aggressive and violent.

It seemed that everywhere Jody went people shied away from him. The entire school, faculty and students, and the surrounding community was wary of the awkward boy with the big nose. Jody had no friends. Not that I ever saw. Jody was bad.

One day on the schoolyard, during an elementary school recess period, Jody turned his sights upon me. Staring at me hard. Frowning angrily as his stare intensified.

I tried to look away. But I was uneasy and glanced at him. This was provocation enough. Without saying a word, he came after me. All the other children moved away. I was a nine-year old kid standing alone. I was scared.

The attack was rapid and startling. With a wild blow to the head Jody knocked me to the ground.

Before I could regain my feet, he was using his body and weight to keep me down, pin me down, grappling me with one hand, and using the fist of his other hand to punch and club me about my head. His fist was fast. All the while he huffed and chortled, giggled and stuttered, emitting angry curses from his mouth.

Methodically he beat me with his raging fist. Struggling against his superior body weight was useless. Jody beat me and pounded my face with solid punches, thudding licks, while he swore and threatened more pain.

I heard him say, "I'll knock you out!"

My face hurt badly. I was very scared. My lips split and tore open, blood ran freely from my mouth and nose. I breathed blood and coughed and gagged. Each punch was an explosion of pain to my head and face.

No adult stepped forward. No one attempted to intervene. Not that I was cognizant of any adult being nearby. I was confused beyond reason. I was a kid and I was being brutally assaulted. It was a terrifying incident. The beating went on and on.

Jody seemed to tire himself out. His fist slowed down. But keeping me pinned down on the asphalt of the playground, he continued striking me with heavy and hard punches from his terrible fist.

Suddenly, dread, anxiety, and fear overwhelmed me. Terror exploded into an incredible fit of fiery anger. Everything happened fast. In absolute blind rage I struggled to lurch myself upward with a strong burst of energy. I went berserk.

With my mouth wide open I seized Jody's big nose with my teeth and bit down hard as I could bite. Jody screamed and howled a horrible cry. His nose felt like a ball of warm meat in my mouth. My teeth clenched tight.

Jody struggled and tried to pull away from me now. But I grabbed his jacket, holding his jacket very tight in my hands. He screamed and struggled and kicked. My teeth held fast to his face.

Finally, he broke free. Ripping away. Just as he tore loose and fled headlong across the schoolyard, I caught quick sight of his wretched face, and I plainly saw a raw clot, a glistening bloody patch where his big nose had been. Out of fear I had bitten his nose off.

After this, Jody let me alone.

One afternoon on a schoolyard baseball diamond, a big kid named Carmichael approached me. He was much bigger than me, and his size was intimidating. With tight setting eyes, and a snout like mouth, Carmichael appeared wolfish. Dread welled inside of me as he came closer and faced me down.

Pushing me, jabbing punches at me, Carmichael boomed with excitement, saying, "Going to your body! Going to your body!" and his punches landed all about my mid-section. His punches became harder and harder. I coughed and groaned and took the pain.

Carmichael laughed. I threw up my hands and attempted to fight back. Carmichael laughed even louder. Tears welled in my eyes. More punches landed and stabbed pain in my abdomen and chest. He was beating me at will. Then, raging anger exploded inside of me.

There was a wooden baseball bat laying in the dust of the diamond. Quickly I moved. Seizing the bat, I swung it with all my young might at Carmichael's hulking head. It landed flush and hard.

Carmichael cried out as the hard wood busted his skull open. He blurted, "Why you hit me?! Why you hit me in the head?!"

I responded with another swing, striking him even harder, this time the bat stroking across the top of his skull. He was stunned on his heels. His small eyes were transfixed in shock.

Carmichael staggered to retain his balance, wobbled on his feet, made a half step sideways, and before he could do anything to recover I gave him another hard swing up against the side of his skull.

Blood appeared from a knot on his head.

The wolf shook himself and dashed away from the scene. I stood on the field with the baseball bat in hand, sighing with relief. I didn't feel good or bad. The whole incident was scary.

I was just glad that I had not been punched and beaten again by the wolf faced Carmichael.

A week or so later I saw Carmichael again. He started towards me, hesitated in his tracks, looked around, and sheepishly he backed off.

I plainly saw his eyes. He knew that I would fight back. But that afforded me little satisfaction. These fights were despairing. The light over these events was not bright.

I recall a darker memory. I remember a day when I was trapped and could not get away. "Fighting back" had not developed in my conscious. Besides, I was not yet strong enough to defend myself. I was too small and too feeble.

I was a five-year-old child and with a group of children at play. We saw two stray dogs copulating in the middle of a dirty Washington, D.C. street. It was a sordid scene. Being there made the world around me seem dark. It was an unclean display and dense with a barren, destitute shade of gray. The air was cold and icy with frost.

An older boy, taller than the rest of us, about twelve years old or so, came along and boisterously jeered and pointed. His voice was very loud, crudely proclaiming the ruttish episode, "Doing the dog!"

Later that day, the very same older boy found me alone. He accosted me. He coaxed and beguiled me to follow him down into the dark and dank basement area of a nearby house. Feeling safe, I smiled and went along.

Cajoling, yet determined, the older boy subdued me, hissing his voice to my face, saying words I had no knowledge of. He was holding me down. And then he imposed his will upon me. I had little strength in my small body. I was five years old. The older boy chanted, "Doing the dog, doing the dog."

The smile fell away from my face.

Pushing the memory into a darker corner became my habit. This was a memory that I tried to erase. But I couldn't. The memory was haunting. Like a ghost on a cold night.

Every flash of my brief memory is ashen. Each dirty frame of my small recollection is smeared to a blur. Try as I might, I could not understand what I had done to let any of this happen. I could not put any reason on the circumstances.

When I looked in the mirror I put on a face. A normal face. I tried to smile. But inside I was broken, and the damage was severe. Peering closely, I could imagine pieces of myself, pummeled to the ground, strewn about, kicked and scattered.

As the memory stayed with me, the meaning of what happened to me became apparent. The pain stayed as well. And then came anger. When the anger was born, I felt sustained.

Having pitted myself in bloody fights with bullies created a feeling of loneliness inside. Defending myself took a lot of emotion.

Yet as my body grew stronger my resolve to defend myself grew stronger as well. Fighting was not something I enjoyed, rather it was a response to my immediate survival.

In time, my spirit of life grew as well. I was making some effort to become balanced. Thoughts and ideas came and developed with each passing day. I wanted to know more about the factors in life that, seemingly, had no understanding in the small world that I knew.

With effort I wondered, 'Where had I come from?' And, 'Why did I have to fend for myself against, what seemed liked, a world full of bullies and tough guys?'

Trusting other people was not easy for me. As I grew, a suspicion of other people grew within me, the motives of others became a curiosity, and I developed trait to be wary and selective. As I matured this trait matured as well. My childhood injuries affected me a great deal.

Coming to terms with the trauma of my past was not without trial. Bad dreams and unpleasant memories have haunted me. I have struggled. I have faltered. I have struggled again

Whenever I started to believe the wound was healed – there was a painful spasm. Distrusting the motives of others was a burden. Always being on guard was exasperating. Searching for an escape route was annoying. But what could one do?

Born into a world of challenge is not so unusual, but all burdens deport a weight that remains unique, exclusive for each one of us as individuals.

Putting the aura of these negatives to rest has been the toughest struggle of my life. Being alone to fend for myself made my labor even tougher.

I wondered with the energy of a hurt child, 'Where are my parents?'

In the early weeks of 1960, my mother was a thirteen-year-old girl, whose given name was Mary Elizabeth, and she was in the early stages of her pregnancy (with me). During that day and time, it was disgraceful for an unmarried thirteen-year-old girl to get pregnant.

What follows is what she told me about this period in her life:

Revealing her condition to her own mother, Bessie Lee White, "Mary Elizabeth," as she was called, was beaten senseless. Slapped. Punched. Hit. Kicked. Beaten until she collapsed. She took it. Verbal abuse followed. Instinctively she cowered and covered herself for protection; protecting me in her womb as well.

When the beating was over, she cleaned herself, frightened at the loss of some blood, but fortunate enough to lick her wounds and recover.

Eight months' pregnant, she turned fourteen years old in June of 1960. But there was no birthday cheer. No celebration. With her fourteen-year-old life skills, she sat secluded inside a dim room and contemplated what lay ahead for her unborn baby and herself.

The physical abuse that had suffered had ceased, but she was still subjected to verbal abuse, profanity ridden name-calling. It was a way of putting her down, keeping her down, and a definitive way of reminding her that she was not a decent young lady. It was a hard bitten and insensible reaction to a serious circumstance.

She was badgered and coerced to place her unborn baby up for foster care or adoption. Blatantly, she was told, "Do not bring that baby home from that hospital! Leave that baby in that hospital!"

Not responding those demands, she was shunned by her family, effectively ostracized.

Only her older sister, my aunt Katherine, provided some aid to my young mother. It had been aunt Katherine who was persistent that my mother be allowed to bring her baby home, and she would not yield her stance. This was a lot for a fourteen-year-old girl to take in.

On Wednesday, 3 August 1960, at 1:07pm, in the city of Washington, D.C., at the District of Columbia General Hospital, my young mother gave birth to me.

She had decided to name me "Gregory", but she could not remember how to spell the name; a maternity nurse on the ward spelled the name for her on the birth certificate form.

Beaten inside the womb I survived to full term. Born now, unwittingly, this was a battle won.

My mother had been alone when she gave birth to me. Racial segregation cast a dense shadow over these events; my maternal grandmother, Bessie Lee White, who was referred to as "Mama," and my aunt Katherine, were not allowed inside the hospital waiting area.

During this era, African-American citizens had to stand outside across the street from the hospital and wait until a birth was complete. Afterward, they could come to a hospital desk and receive news of a birth and sometimes visit the patient. Mama and Katherine had come.

Ironically, Mama had been strongly against my mother bringing me home from the hospital, but now she relented and allowed my mother to bring me home. Afterword, she softened more with each with each passing day.

Three days after my birth, with me wrapped and bundled in hospital issued garb, after gathering her scant few possessions, my fourteen-year-old mother took me from the District of Columbia General Hospital and out into the world.

My mother's childhood went out the back door - just as my childhood passed through the front door. Together, into the 1960's we went.

During the first week after my birth my mother fretted with worry. She was penniless. Unemployed. And, during her pregnancy, she had been coerced to drop out of the seventh grade in junior high school.

She was desperate for "baby things" and money necessary to purchase these "things."

Anxiety poured over her, and my young mother decided to confront the seventeen-year-old high school youth who was my father. The boy who had "gotten her into trouble" as it was called in those days.

Without immediate help or consistent support she worried that we would not survive for long. At least not together. She had a fear that she may have to let me go for foster care; as had been strongly suggested.

Taking me with her, she walked from her family home at 3520 10th Street NW to the family home of my father at 1312 Spring Road NW in the District of Columbia. Holding herself up steady, committing herself, she knocked on the door to the house on Spring Road NW.

My paternal grandmother, Mrs. Ruth Archie, answered the door and let my mother inside. She told my mother that her son, Frank Clifton, "Clift" as he was known, was not home now.

My mother opened up and explained that her son, Clift, was the father of her baby. My grandmother was open and understanding.

My mother went on to explain that she was destitute and in need of help and support for the newborn baby. She told my grandmother where she lived on 10th Street and wrote down the address on a piece of paper.

With compassion, my grandmother listened intently, gave my mother some money for milk and diapers, and assured my mother that she would discuss the entire matter with her husband, James Eugene Archie, when he arrived home from work later that day. My grandmother encouraged her not to worry.

When my grandmother told my grandfather that "Clift has a baby by a girl around the corner on 10th Street," immediately my grandfather wanted to know the all the details, he wanted to know the name of this girl and where this girl lived.

He was taken off guard, surprised by this turn of events, but his concern was genuine. Right away he wanted to know the details of what was going on.

My grandmother gave him the piece of paper with the address.

Address in hand, my grandfather walked the four blocks to the house on 10th Street. Knocking on the door, introducing himself, he asked my mother, "Let me see the baby?" She took him upstairs in the house to the bedroom where I was sleeping on a bed.

My grandfather looked at me, picked me up for a few minutes, and said, 'He's an Archie, don't worry, Clift will take care of this baby. This baby looks just like Clift."
And with that, days after I was born, my teenage father, my paternal grandparents, and his immediate family came into my life. Grandma and grandpa took to me right away.

There was some short talk of my parents getting married, which was something of a custom in those days. But it did not happen. They remained a steady couple for five years or so.

Going their separate ways, they remained good friends – lifelong friends. Their mutual connection was raising me best they could. My parents were little more than children. My parents were forever young.

Even in knowing this brief of family history, the question lingered in my head, 'Where are my parents?'

My parents, still living with their own parents, went to work very soon after I was born. Rarely did I have time with my parents during a work week. And so, as child I was primarily cared for by Mama during the week, and by Grandma on weekends and holidays.

Without fail, my father or his father, Grandpa, would come and get me every Friday afternoon and take me to the family home. First on Spring Road NW, and later relocated to 1921 Otis Street NE. It was the Otis Street household that would be my foundation for growth and learning.

My school days were being squandered. I spent a great deal of time reading, but I wouldn't say that I was a very good reader. If that makes sense. But reading allowed me a window to the rest of the world. I read about all manner of subjects.

No doubt, comic books were a mainstay of my young piecemeal, makeshift literary diet. I devoured comic books.

Again, I was not a great reader, but a constant reader; tenacious in working my way through a story, and unknowingly nurturing a desire to become a better reader. I did this one word at a time. Having an old piece of a dictionary on hand became commonplace.

Reading was the rapture, and the initial positive in my young life. I remember hording books and magazines and burrowing myself away from the world around me. This was my escape.

With reading came learning. No way to separate one entity from the other. I discovered the diversity of history and languages. I began to note the many cultures and religions of people around the world. It amazed me that there was so much more to the world-at-large than what I saw around me in D.C.

I found encyclopedia's and World Almanac's fascinating, intriguing, and favored reading material. National Geographic and various travel magazines were also a preferred choice.

After reading an adventurous article, an insightful passage, or informative essay, I would get excited and feel an urgency to discover more. The rest of the world held an interest of unlimited possibilities.

Geography appealed to me in a great way. Facts and information about other countries was engaging. I developed a great interest in how these nations and states came to be.

I would read about other places, faraway locales, foreign and exotic areas of the world, and I would daydream and reverie and imagine just how exciting it would be to travel to these faraway places.

At this point in time I had very little idea of how I would reach these faraway places. I suppose I had a notion that I would work, save my money and travel. The novel idea of traveling was a great way to fill a young mind.

Story by story, I learned about various ways and means of travel. Soon I was associating my experience on "Pirate Lake" with the greater world of boats and ships. Seafaring and maritime were key words that gave me a route for reference.

I discovered great tales of adventure and intrigue. Stories about the lives of sailors appealed to me in a great way. And I read all that I could find.

What I read and what I learned was not always the ritzy, neither was the prestigious. A sailor's experience, from what I had learned up this point, was not one without challenge. Being a sailor was a rough life. Many would claim that it was a coarse life.

Sailor's, by age old accounts, were hard bitten men and women who accustomed themselves to tough conditions, harsh meals, and loneliness. What made this all bearable was the romance and the desire.

The simple idea of leaving the world behind was daring. Going somewhere far away was exciting. The deep blue sea held a mystique of danger and a lure of beauty, it was uncanny and graceful, and I wanted to be there. No matter the odds.

I would close my eyes, and pledge a short vow to myself, "I'm going."

CHAPTER TWO

When I was seventeen years old I walked past a United States Navy recruiting office. I looked inside.

Twice before I had been rebuffed and turned away from enlisting in the U.S. Navy. I did not have a high school diploma. But I wanted to join. I desired to see the rest of the world. I had read so much about other places, far away locales, and all about the many foreign and exotic areas of the world.

I would daydream and imagine just how exciting it would be to travel to these distant places. I longed to venture overseas. I wanted to know these foreign places face to face. At this point in my life I had very little idea of how I would reach these faraway places, yet the desire inside was overwhelming, the longing was an aching feeling.

I was nobody special in Washington, D.C. I had to get away from this place. With what I thought was a good method, or good reasoning, I had desperately waged a tough fight within myself to bury my past. I wanted to forget my entire childhood. Too many unpleasant scenes had occurred.

What better way to reinvent myself than to run fast and far? My body was strong and full of life. I could run like the wind.

I straightened myself and went through door to the recruiting office.

The recruiter, a tall African American man, welcomed me inside. His dress white uniform was starched and pressed with narrow creases and fixed with ribbons and small silver colored anchors that had a star.

He was a Senior Chief Petty Officer. He shook my hand. He talked. I listened. I was nervous. Not having a high school diploma caused me to sweat and brace myself for rejection. I had been in the 8th grade for three years.

The Senior Chief reasoned that he would enlist me into military service on the condition that I do well on the examinations that he would arrange for me to take, with an added note that I pursue a General Education Diploma, GED, within my first year of service.

He said that he would credit me for attempting to enroll in the 9th grade in school. He said that would help. I agreed. My only request was that I be assigned to a ship and have sea duty. I did not want shore duty. Going to sea was my goal.

All I possessed were the clothes on my back, an 8th grade education, and a five-dollar bill in my pocket. Nothing else. With what I thought was good reason I had desperately waged a fight within myself to bury my past.

Joining the U.S. Navy was my ticket to the rest of the world. I wanted to leave the life of poverty behind me. There were holes in my shoes. Scarcely, I sustained myself on one meal a day. A makeshift meal of hot dogs and canned goods. A piece of soap and a place to wash myself was a rarity. Being poor was burdensome, and it seemed to be only getting worse.

Really, I lived wherever a family member would take me in. I wanted to deny it, but I lived on the street sometimes. Laundry rooms and vacant buildings was where I frequently found shelter. In time I learned to deal with it.

No one would miss me.

Appraising me and giving a nod, the Senior Chief promised me sea duty. He asked me about my parents. I told him that I was on my own.

Speaking in a low voice I said, "My parents don't care about me. I been on my own, on the street." I thought about telling him more, but I didn't. I was nervous and didn't want to blow any chance I had to enlist.

I waged a fight within myself to bury my past.

Willing myself, the road forward was my only focus. It was the road forward that would save me.

I sat stiffly in a chair next to the recruiter's desk and took a deep breath and a sigh.

It was obvious that I was a bum. My clothes were wrinkled, and I kept shifting me eyes, looking down at the holes in my shoes.

The Senior Chief followed me eyes, looking at my raggedy shoes, said he understood and that he would help me. I was still scared. He did a lot of paperwork and put a stack of papers before me. I signed all the papers with my name.

Two weeks later I was on my way.

After midnight, the 747-airplane touched down in Orlando, Florida. Hastening along with all the other passengers I disembarked the airplane quickly.

This had been my first time aboard an airplane. Milling about, U.S. Navy recruits were everywhere. Wide eyed and alert, joined the mass of fresh young faces near the baggage area. I had no luggage. Just the five-dollar bill in my pocket.

We were given directions to "go this way" or "go that way." Even at this early hour the sense of energy was throughout the airport. I had never been inside an airport, but I hustled along, following directions given to me.

Navy drill instructors were waiting for us. Up until this point it had all seemed distant, not something that I could touch, but when the drill instructors herded me into the ranks of other new recruits I had a feeling of "this is it" overcome me.

Exhausted from the journey, yet full of excitement and expectation of what was to come. My optimism peaked to the max.

Finally, I was in the United States Navy! I was going to be a sailor!

Recruit Training Unit 237. Mess Management Specialist, Petty Officer First Class Burgess, and Mess Management Specialist Chief Petty Officer Simon were the two Non-Commissioned Officers, career military service members, assigned to the task of training and drilling us; entrusted to reshaping our way of thinking, and transforming each one of us into United States Navy sailors.

Usually, eight or nine training units started their basic training at the same time, hence these training units would complete training at the same time. Three of the training units were comprised of female recruits.

A well-intended performance competition of sorts among the collective training units, a system of grading and scoring points.

Some of the categories for points included the team effort of: physical training (PT), maintaining proper military uniform, marching and drilling, keeping the barracks clean, having gear and racks (beds) properly stowed and made neat, small arms training, shipboard orientation and safety, and classroom instruction and examinations.

There were flags awarded to a training unit for competence regarding these inspections, drills, and performance of events. Earning a flag emboldened with an "I" would indicate competence for infantry training (marching), and a streaming red ribbon was attached each time the training unit successfully passed an inspection or won out in an event.

Toward the end of seven weeks of basic training, the week leading on to graduation day, the training unit with the most flags and ribbons would be honored with the Commanding Officer's Award for Excellence.

It was a ceremonial styled white flag with gold fringes and trim. We talked about that a lot, it was a competition of sorts, and it was a trophy to behold.

For raw kids, some of us who came from unstable backgrounds, earning this distinguished flag represented the value of team work, the will inside each one of us, and the earnest desire to accomplish something worthwhile.

We were kids that were having the time of our lives. Being a sailor was likened to being prince. At least for me it was. The expectation of a bright future was thrilling.

An All-American lot we were, white guys and black guys, Hispanic kids and Asian kids, city boys and country boys. Each one of us with a story – a story that had lead each one of us to this "grinder" beneath hot August sun of Orlando, Florida.

Camaraderie was at an all-time high. Everyone got along with each other. Everyone looked out for each other. We shared a common bond. Our ambition, our specific goal was to complete our training with high standards, pass through this interim stage, be issued our orders for duty, join the ships of the United States Navy Fleet, and carry the title of "sailor" wherever we went.

Eight weeks went by swift enough. Out on the "grinder," beneath the scorching hot Florida Sun, the tarry asphalt of the "grinder" softened the rubber soles of our "boondocker" boots. We marched and drilled. Right away, cadence was called, and we repeated the chant of cadence in unison.

A lot of physical training (PT) took place; the marching, the run of the obstacle course, the push-up's, and the strenuous exercise of the "eight-count body builders."

Standing close together in the "gas chamber" we endured tear gas training and felt our eyes sting and burn until we were laughing at the willful toughness that reaped through our pains. First Aid training. Shipboard firefighting training. Man-overboard and sea survival exercises.

There was a week of "work week" where, in the scullery, we washed more pots and pans than I had ever seen. On the weapons ranged we fired .45 caliber semi-automatic pistols.

On the mess decks I had never seen so much food. We ate all the chow we wanted to eat. All the food was full of color, hot and appetizing, and it was spread along a long row of a chow line like nothing I had seen before.

Back inside our barracks, in the crew lounge area during the evenings, cigarettes were smoked and letters from home were read. Everyone had a story. Many of us shared thoughts and ideas and dreams of what the future held for us once we were out of boot camp and into the ranks of the fleet.

We took photographs and talked about our girlfriends (a few of the guys were married and they talked of family and such).

I had no girlfriend, and for the most part I listened to the other guys. Listening to the others speak about female relationships was a growing lesson of sorts. How relationships developed and maintained was always interesting.

In contrast to the life I had left behind in D.C. there was no tension, no disharmonious vibe was in the atmosphere. I recall there were no serious arguments, everyone seemed to get along with each other.

Being in boot camp I felt, for the first time outside my home, that I was in place that was a safety zone.

Without plan or expectation of benefit, we were forming bonds of friendship that would last and bear the test of time. Without sham we were young and we were going to win. We all knew it. We were going to win. The taste of winning was in the air all around us.

One week before we were to graduate from boot camp, we learned that we had scored several points above all the other Training Unit's and that we had duly earned the coveted "white and gold fringed" flag that represented the "Commanding Officer's Award for Excellence."

With that distinction we were considered the top performing training unit of our class.

My friends while in boot camp, were Carroll Farmer, Perry, Billings, and Padilla. Carroll Farmer was a white kid with large ears from South Carolina, and I remember having an easy bond with him.

Farmer and I became friends from the start. Perry and Billings were black kids from Mississippi and Georgia respectively.

Perry and I would talk a lot about Jackson, the city where he hailed from. Padilla was a rotund Hispanic kid from San Antonio, and I recall him being full of life and open for friendship.

Good naturedly, Billings, from Georgia, was the newfound friend who gave me the nickname "Reptile" because I had this serious heat rash, and because I was a good swimmer. (I use their real names here in hopes that they will find me, and we can re-kindle our friendships).

On our very first "Liberty Call" as sailors, we were permitted to venture into Orlando and the surrounding areas of the city after our graduation from boot camp. A lot of guys and young ladies went to Disney World or Sea World.

My small group of friends decided that wasn't for us. We were legitimate sailors now. We felt that we had earned something that possessed an edge. Asking around, we put out questions like, "Where is the 'real action' in this town?"

"Orange Blossom Trail," was always the answer.

Scrubbed clean. Ready for the world. Every single day at 4pm we were showered, dressed, and gone. We hit that first Liberty Call like there was no tomorrow.

For the long weekend after recruit's graduation we hit "OBT", as Orange Blossom Trail was called, and we jumped and tramped from nightclub to nightclub. We stomped from bar to bar. We staggered from strip club to strip club.

I remember names of places that are likely long gone: "THE ABC LOUNGE, THE BOOBY TRAP LOUNGE, THE CENTERFOLD BAR & LOUNGE and EVIL PEOPLE," and some others.

For a green, young sailor fresh out of boot camp OBT was the place to be. Sure, we were green, but the lessons we learned were a definitive reality. This was our "rite of passage" into the ranks of being an American sailor.

With this long weekend of celebration behind us we were committed to remain at the Naval Training Center for two week of Advance Training (AT). I had chosen to become an Engineman. My specific training would be for the Engineering Department aboard a U.S. Navy ship.

Two full weeks in Advance Training became an 8am to 4pm schedule. It was classroom and vocational work. In my class we were orientated and taught the basic ways of a Main Engine Room (MER) aboard a U.S. Navy war ship.

I had a strong desire and interest in mechanics and the nuts and bolts of taking things apart and putting them back together again.

Being an Engineman would suit me well. Machinery, pumps, boilers, and engines. All sounded great to me and I looked forward to taking on the challenge of learning all that I could. The weekends were free time and "Liberty Call" was the order of the day.

Each weekend was spent exploring Orlando, shopping, taking in a movie, dining out, and learning what it was to be a young adult. Not that any of us projected outstanding social skills. But we were finding our way one step at a time.

We shared stories, often spoke of family and girlfriends, and many of us had an idea, if not a story of how we had found our way into the U.S. Navy. Everyone had a reason and such a story. My own such story was simple enough, and I kept close a reverie regarding my own inspirations, only sharing the details with one or two good friends.

What began as a childhood game, a summertime diversion, a lark and a makeshift way to shape curiosity and imagination into a piecemeal form of reality.

Closing my eyes, I remembered the key event in my formative years that turned my eye toward the sailor's life. I would smile.

With clear memory, I thought of just how special it was when I had been playing on our childhood Pirate Lake in the old fiberglass bathtub liner with my young friends. It was a genuine reverie. In this manner I would keep my eyes closed for long, quiet moments.

Duty orders and assignments came and were passed out among all of us, the new sailors, fresh faced and prepared. Guys were being sent to destinations to different parts of the country and all over the world.

Some of these locations I had never heard of, not until now, and I thought all this was very exciting. Some of the new orders noted place such as: Diego Garcia, Roosevelt Roads, Rota, Spain and La Spezia, Italy.

My own orders carried what seemed to be notes and a list of strange sounding names: "Ingalls LITTON INDUSTRIES Pascagoula, MS US NAV Pre-Comm USS Moosbrugger DD-980, Charleston, SC, Engineering Dept. Fireman FA."

I was going to be stationed aboard a new Spruance-Class destroyer. The "Pre-Comm" on my orders indicated that I would be awaiting commissioning of this ship. I would be part of the original crew.

Yet, I was still green. I didn't know what most of these words and acronyms meant, nor did I understand the significance of being part of an "original ship's crew. All I comprehended was I was going to be on the newest war ship in the U.S. Fleet. Life had changed in a significant way. The future looked promising. Meeting new people, making new friends, and learning the way of a ship was very exciting.

My limited social skills were being cast aside one at a time. A sense of belonging to something more immense than the community in which I had come from did not go without notice. Slowly my demeanor as a shy and callow youth was beginning to dissipate. I was still skinny and green, but I was growing.

Carroll Farmer and Padilla were my initial "strip club" partners. We would drink and revel with the dancers. Back in those days if a kid was wearing a military uniform alcohol was served without any question about age and served with a smile. Glasses of vodka and beers stacked and covered our tables.

We were all sharp in our dress white uniforms and highly polished black leather shoes. There was a strip joint called "Evil People" that my small group of guys became regular, front row patrons at.

In short time, I became acquainted a couple of dancers that worked at "The Booby Trap". They gorgeous looking young women, as were all dancers at strip clubs. Two of them were white and one of them was black; not that it mattered, but just to paint a picture and give life and effect to an old memory.

These young women were about 21 years old, they were on their own, making their way as dancers or strippers. Becoming acquainted with them was pleasant enough.

The young women offered me marijuana and made and spoke of "dropping a tab" of acid or LSD. I accepted the reefer. I declined the acid. Though I was fresh faced and raw, I was cautious and watchful, and I had seen a few things on the streets of Washington, D.C. that kept me on my toes. Acid was something I had heard bad stories about.

One night at the club, Diane, one of the young woman I had taken an interest in, gave me a slip of paper with her telephone number and address. In my car during a "lap dance" she told me to call and we could meet later. She was a long-haired brunette, very attractive, and I looked forward to making a serious connection with her.

The next day we spoke over the phone. She asked me if I wanted to come over and hang out and smoke some reefer. I said "yes." And then she asked me to bring my friend Farmer along so that he could keep her girlfriend and roommate company.

Her roommate was named Crystal, and she was a dancer at the club as well. Anyway, I told Farmer what the deal was, and he agreed to go along. He was eager to see Crystal, and he smiled when I told him the plan that Diane and I had made.

It was an early Saturday afternoon when Farmer and I showed up at the bungalow style house where Diane and Crystal lived. I remember it being a hot day in Florida (and that's real hot).

There we were the four of us, Crystal and Farmer sitting together on a sofa, Diane and myself sitting close together on a love seat in the living room of the house. A shoe box filled to the brim with reefer was on the coffee table, and we were smoking thick rolled joints. A gallon of vodka was on the table as well. I had not smoked any reefer in almost a year.

The powerful reefer had me stoned in a matter of minutes. Mild hallucinations began to claim my senses. We were all getting spaced out. Diane was sitting close and she felt good. Maybe I was going to spend the night here, this crossed my mind when we started kissing and making out.

Things were getting heavy and taking place fast. Diane and I were kissing and grabbing each other. I was stoned out of my mind, and it was feeling good.

Suddenly, I heard the loud roar of motors. The thundering roar of several motors being revved up was loud enough to make the small house seem to tremble.

I was so high I ignored the loud sound of the motors. I dismissed the vibrations. The commotion was coming from outside on the street. Not my concern.

Diane jumped to her feet and said, "I'll be right back," and hurriedly went out the front door of the bungalow. I kept on smoking reefer and drinking vodka. Farmer and the other young woman were making out, heedless of Diane and myself.

I was spaced out, still smoking reefer. I kept hearing the loud thunder of all these motors being revved up. I had a feeling that I better check and see where Diane went.

When I peered out the living room window I saw Diane standing in the street and engaged in an animated conversation with this guy on a Harley-Davidson motorcycle.

All I could see was a horde of motorcycles up and down the street. There were at least 30 hard core looking bikers perched on motorcycles in the street. It was a motorcycle gang!

My eyes flew open wide in shock. My mind went cold sober. I broke and ran through the house into the kitchen for the backdoor, all the while shouting the alarm to my partner, "Farmer! It's a motorcycle gang! It's a motorcycle gang!"

Farmer jumped to his feet, his eyes wide and alarmed.

The backdoor was locked. It was a lock that required a key to unlock it – even from the inside of the door. With my mind fogged from smoking reefer and my judgement marred, I panicked. I kicked the door down.

Farmer was right on my heels as we charged down the alley behind the house, our feet beat hard against the pavement as we ran, never looking back.

We had no interest in an encounter with a motorcycle gang. We ran for several blocks until we flagged down a taxi cab. When it was over we breathed easier and laughed about the entire episode. I didn't smoke reefer for a long time afterwards.

Life was moving fast now. With military orders in hand, sea bag over our shoulders, we left the U.S. Navy Recruit Training Command in Orlando, Florida and spread ourselves across the country, throughout the fleet, and around the world.

I had only been away from home for three months, but there were notable changes in the way the life at home appeared. It was a feeling of great energy that suggested the differences.

I was still green, just beginning to spread my wings, but already life was taking a new shape and was developing with excitement.

The few sights that I had seen in Florida, the new people that I had met, the thrills that my new friends and I had shared running up and down Orange Blossom Trail, all these factors made me eager and ready to find more adventure.

When I left Orlando, Florida and went home on "Leave" to Washington, D.C. the future seemed bright.

Just as I had dreamed, I was a returning home as a sailor. Having a good career in the U.S. Navy was the primary ambition of my young life. It was an ambition that generated a great feeling.

As I traveled and made my way from airport to airport, I thought about what I had told my recruiter, the Senior Chief, when I had quietly yet clearly said to him concerning my parents. I had told him, "My parents don't care about me. I been on my own, on the street."

In my estimation, it was true. I stayed away. There had been unpleasant scenes. I had not been encouraged nor supported to achieve much as child and into my adolescence.

But this was not true.

Like many other insecure, coming of age, young people I saw my parents as the root of all my problems. And "yes" there was a film of insecurity casting a discolored picture over what I saw or thought that I saw.

Loud voices, negative sounds, nearly always berating me, deriding me, and pushing me aside with a swearing. Several times when the door had been locked – with me standing outside with no place to go. Is it any wonder that I knew the streets so well?

With these ideas inside my head, I turned away from bonding with family and old friends. The scenes from an unfulfilled childhood captured my imagination, and I felt there was something missing when in the company of those who should have been closest to me.

I had only been away from home for three months, but there were notable changes in the way the life at home appeared.

But at the time I didn't think much about it. My life had changed. I was headed for the comfort and balm of sunshine and blue sky. The deep blue sea awaited. I would meet her in a grand way.

The few sights that I had seen in Florida, the new people I had met, the thrills that my new friends and I had shared running up and down Orange Blossom Trail, all these factors made me eager and ready to find more adventure.

I was ready to get back to seeing the rest of the world. Being back in Washington, D.C. was not what I wanted.

Just the idea of going to join a brand-new U.S. Navy ship was exciting. A great expectation welled inside me. And I was ready for it all. I was 18 years old now. I had a few dollars in my pocket now. And I had my beloved sea bag.

When I arrived in Mobile, Alabama I was met by a U.S. Navy driver who took me and another young sailor to Pascagoula, Mississippi. In Florida I had been centrally located in Orlando and had not traveled about.

The shelter of being in the U.S. Navy was comforting. I assumed that being a U.S. service member granted me some security, how much security I was not certain, but there was a sense of safety among other sailors.

But now, I was traveling by automobile from Mobile to Pascagoula, and it was as "deep south" as one could get. The only place south of this area was the Gulf of Mexico and the expanse of the sea.

What I knew of the deep south I had learned from books and magazines and news reports; just as I had learned about pretty much everything else.

The media had depicted Alabama and Mississippi, and other areas of the deep south, as an unjust or violent apartheid region of the country. In contrast to Washington, D.C. this area of the country was another world. Yet, growing up in the city of D.C. had groomed me to avoid neighborhoods and areas where potential trouble may arise.

Black neighborhoods or white neighborhoods, trouble was trouble. Getting jumped and beaten was all the same. And I didn't want to get caught up in anything negative. I stayed away from secluded areas. There was no need in taking any undue chances. But I didn't want to think about social issues and politics.

I only wanted to hit town after town, port after port, and duly locate the next "Orange Blossom Trial" and the "real action" in whatever town or port.

I felt good about life and the world around me. And I was young and ready to take on all the "gin joints" and sailor's dives in the world.

In Pascagoula I was taken to a U.S. Navy barracks where I met my fellow shipmates; we were scheduled to stay in this barracks for two weeks before moving aboard our new ship the USS Moosbrugger DD-980 (after we moved aboard the ship we had another four weeks in the shipyard).

Everything went well during this six-week period. For the most part I stayed close to the barracks, drank beer when off duty, listened to my radio and tape player, and read magazines.

It was a slow and easy environment. The weather in southern Mississippi was real nice. I remember having the warmth of the sun make me feel good inside.

Moving onboard my first ship, the USS MOOSEBRUGGER DD-980, a Spruance-Class Destroyer, a definitive "Man-O-War" ship, I was assigned to a "rack" (a bunk) in the Engineering Department berthing compartment.

I was also informed that I would be taking on Fireman duties in MER-2, that is Main Engine Room 2. All young sailors with a Fireman rank were dubbed as a "bilge rat" due to the dirty, mucky work of the billet, and it was a badge of honor.

The Engineering berthing compartment was known as "Snipes Castle". "Snipe" is Navy slang for a sailor in the Engine Department.

Within "Snipes Castle" there was an area, one small section where I had my rack, that was known as "Shit Can Alley" (because there was a trash can there), and because we were a rag tag, grimy group of sailors.

These guys were my shipmates and friends: Seckinger, Dutch, Depas, Jonesy, Schultz, Totoris, Kloepper, Bingham and a few others. M-Division was our division and we mustered in ranks every morning on the helo deck.

Within days of being on the ship I learned that there was going to be a Commissioning Ceremony, a big deal, on 16 December 1978.

We were the first crew, the original crew, and we would have the distinction of having the title "Plank Owner" granted to each one of us.

Even more, we were issued a "plank" piece of wood board with our names engraved on brass name plate, a ceremonial "Plank Owner" certificate, and a USS Moosbrugger DD-980 ball cap – with the emboldened word "Plank Owner" on the back of the cap.

So here I am, a kid with a few new titles and moniker's (some of which I had to learn the meaning of), "Sailor, Fireman Apprentice, Snipe, Bilge rat, and Plank owner, Snipes Castle, and Shit Can Alley."

Still a teenager, and a man of the world, in certain terms, and being aboard the 'Moose was a dream come true. What else could I imagine.

Serving aboard a brand new ship, with a brand new lease on a life that had not always been held in the light of success. And we all prepared to sail the high seas.

When the Commissioning Ceremony was performed, we were duly told that we would be disembarking and sailing for Charleston, South Carolina in a matter of days. And we were told of a schedule for the ship, with visits where we would call at two seaports.

We would sail through the Gulf of Mexico into the Caribbean Sea, and on into the expanse of the Atlantic Ocean. We would have a liberty call at Port Au Prince, Republic of Haiti, and a second liberty call at Charlotte Amalie, Saint Thomas in the U.S. Virgin Islands.

Port Au Prince would be our first foreign port of call. That makes it forever special in my young experience as a sailor. The "first cut is the deepest" as the saying goes.

From a page or chapter in the numerous books I had read about foreign places, I knew some historical aspects about Haiti. The biographies of Toussaint L'Overture and the Emperor Jean-Jacques Dessalines.

To know these names was to learn that Haiti was a country that was predominately populated of people who descended from a once heavily colonized area of Africa, known as French West Africa.

During colonial times, in Haiti there had been a revolt against slavery, not merely an uprising, but a war against the French Army of Napoleon Bonaparte. More recent history exposed brief articles about President Francois Duvalier and his son Jean Claude Duvalier.

This was a history that I had only read about. Now I was here on location, and that was exciting.

CHAPTER THREE

One day, in the open air up on the main deck of the 'Moose, Starboard side, I met a guy from New York City named Bruce Clark. We shared a few comments on how things were going and such.

Over the next few days Bruce and I would see each around the ship, speak to each other and chat some small talk. We seemed to share a few ideas in common. We became friends. We became partners.

The 'Moose dropped anchor in the Port Au Prince Bay. The water was the clearest light blue color that I had ever seen. The water reminded me of blue gems that I had only seen in museums. There were small boats carrying old men and young boys that sailed or rowed out to meet our ship.

These small vessels were beaten and worn, some made of rough looking metal and other boats fashioned from the roughhewn of wood. "Bum boats" they were called, and these vessels were stocked full of all kinds of wooden carvings, statues, walking sticks, busts and other hand carvings.

Everything they had was hand cut, shaped and crafted with skill. The carving of the wood pieces was unlike anything I had ever seen.

From the rail of our ship, sailors tossed coins and bills to the young boys, who in turn began to dive and swim like fish pursuing coins through that beautiful blue water. With the rise of mountains in the backdrop, the bay that lined Port Au Prince was an elegant body of water.

All the sailors on the ship were called to quarters for muster and we were given a speech about what to do, what not to do, and where not to venture when we went ashore and into Port Au Prince.

For many of us, especially those of us fresh out of boot camp, this would be our first time visiting a foreign country. We were strictly advised not to violate any laws in Haiti (or there would be grave consequences). Don't drink the water. Don't eaten certain meats.

Venereal disease was rampant, and the final warning was concerning Voo Doo. We were told not to go to any Voo Doo show alone; go in groups.

Bruce and I decided that we would be a two man group. When Bruce and I stepped onto the pier and walked along the dock in Port Au Prince we were swallowed amidst a sea of talking faces.

Black people were everywhere. This was another world. But for our clothing and mannerisms we fit right into with the masses. The sun was high overhead and hot. Everywhere people were milling and rushing, laughing and smiling, their voices aloud with Creole and French words.

It was fascinating to be beneath the sun in some far away land.

Before I could think much about what was happening, Bruce and I were standing next to this gypsy taxi cab and a young looking driver. I wanted to remember the face of the driver in case anything negative went down. He looked like a regular guy, smooth brown face, about my own height.

In good English, the driver encouraged us into his small taxi. His promise was to drive us anywhere we wished to go. All night. For five dollars.

Bruce and I looked at each other. Was this guy for real? To be fair, we gave him ten dollars.

From the window of the taxi cab I watched the landscape as it sped along through the streets of Port Au Prince. Sights of abject poverty were everywhere. The blight of the city made stark contrast to the attitude and manners of the people we saw. Everyone I encountered seemed open and friendly.

The driver zipped his way through the streets with skill and knowing. We had told him that we wanted to be taken someplace where "the action" was. We wanted to drink and have a good time and meet some women.

After driving about for maybe 30 minutes or so, we finally pulled to a stop on this dirt and rubble strewn street. A huge crater of a hole was in the middle of this street. People were out on throngs, selling stuff, buying things.

Children ran and played. The scene was colorful and held life that seemed uncomplicated and without burden. But that was clearly a "false positive" for there was the poverty, there was the struggle to sustain oneself from day to day. And that drew a picture that was complex.

Initially, I thought we may have to ask the driver to take us somewhere else, this didn't look like the kind of scene or "the action" that we were seeking. Bruce and I exchange a look. The driver beckoned for us to get out and follow him. Bruce and I complied.

Following the driver, we entered this house looking building and took a dark corridor. We walked past several closed doors on both sides of this narrow passage. I was getting suspicious about where this brother was leading us, then suddenly, we stepped back outside.

Met by music that was loud. It was a courtyard full of people. Brightly colored lights were swinging from electrical cords. There was a long bar made of patches of wood.

But the courtyard was dominated by a large dance floor that was ringed with good looking young women sitting in chairs. There were at least fifty women in those chairs.

It was a nightclub with dancing, and there was a grand bar. Dim red lighting reflected off several large mirrors in the place. Around the club I saw that many of our shipmates were already there.

A fair number of Chief Petty Officer's and Line Officer's caroused around the joint and drinking alongside the enlisted sailors. The music was loud, the party was alive, and everyone was having a good time. This was "the action" that we sought. The name of the place was "The Washington Club."

Back on the ship and at sea we sailed for Charlotte Amalie, Saint Thomas, U.S. Virgin Islands. It was a short sail from Haiti. Again, Bruce I and I hit the port city. It was the time of our lives. We did some shopping. We ate in some small restaurants. Rented moped scooters and rode fast as we could around the island. We met some young people and joined then at a cookout and a softball game. The young women there treated us real nice.

For the most part, Bruce and I made no real plans about what we would do. We were "winging it" so to speak; checking out the sights, getting something to eat, meeting new people. In the night life we would mingle and party in bars and nightclubs, meeting young women was always interesting.

Being optimistic, we remained ready to explore, enjoying life as it came. Much later in the night, when the Sun has long set, we discovered, once again, where "the action" was. Being young sailors, we wanted to take on the world.

Some of the places we visited in our travels were:

Charlotte Amalie, Saint Thomas, U.S.V.I.

Port Au Prince, Haiti.

Guantanamo Bay, Cuba.

Roosevelt Roads, Puerto Rico.

Charleston, South Carolina.

Moss Point, Mississippi.

Biloxi, Mississippi.

New Orleans, Louisiana.

Fort Lauderdale, Florida.

Miami, Florida.

It was in Port Everglades, or Fort Lauderdale, I happened to meet up with a guy that I had known from back home. His name was Brian Bell.

The ship was docked in Port Everglades and Bruce and I had liberty call. We were hanging out on Sea Breeze Drive inside an Amusement Arcade when I noticed this guy, a brother about my own age, looking my way with some intensity. His face was familiar

.

Strange that I would recognize someone this far from home. I walked over, and we started talking. I knew this guy. We talked some more and made the connection. There had been a time when we were both detained by the police.

Remarkably, he had escaped from a juvenile detention center (in the Washington, D.C. area) and made his way to Florida by taking Trailways Bus and hitchhiking rides. This was still in the '70s and hitching a ride along a highway was still kind of cool.

Together, Brian, Bruce and myself, we left the arcade and took a walk along the strip in Fort Lauderdale. It was night time. The beach was on the opposite of the street.

Brian told Bruce and I about how he had been committed to serve 6 months in the juvenile detention center, and how it had been an awful, oppressive experience. So, he had decided to escape. And one evening after dark he had climbed a 12 foot fence topped with barbed wire and "ran" into the thick of wood that surrounded the detention center.

While he recanted his story, I could not help but think of all the African slaves that had "ran" into the night in pursuit of freedom. And I remembered that I had a friend, who went by the name of George Carter, who had likewise escaped from a juvenile youth center. My friend George had hidden out on the neighborhood for several weeks until he was caught and taken back to the detention center.

This was a bold move. Escape from captivity was always brash and defiant. Bruce and I looked at each other and we knew that Brian had a lot of heart, and we admired him. We went into a liquor store and got a bottle of whiskey. Walking over to the beach area, we could see the ocean and surf, and the breeze was warm.

Brian was incredulous when I told him of how I had become a sailor in the U.S. Navy. He was excited at the idea of being in the military. He asked Bruce and myself over and over, "Do you think they will let me join?"

We thought that there may be a chance for Brian. After all, I had enlisted without completing high school. We encouraged him to return home, find someone to help and advise him, his parents, his church, his teachers or maybe a coach or counselor from school. Likely, and it was possible, a juvenile court judge would grant him some respite. Brian listened intently.

We chatted about his situation into the early hours of the new day. Brian vowed that he was going to turn himself in to the police, get some help, and try his best to join the military. I knew he was sincere. I could see it in his face.

When the sun began to rise high in the eastern sky, Bruce and I gave Brian some money, wished him good luck, shook hands, and we returned to our ship. Brian headed north on Sea Breeze Drive.

Back on the USS Moosbrugger I settled into working in Main Engine Room #2. The engine room was huge, as one could imagine, and it was filled in every corner and space with machinery and pumps and electronic equipment. It was hot in the engine room. And it was always loud and full of noise (from the action of the machines).

Engineering sailors would don "hearing protection" in the form of either ear plugs or "Mickey Mouse ears" (which covered the entire ear. I wore the "Mickey Mouse ears."

Engineering Department Watch consisted of several sailors on duty. Commissioned Officers and Chief Petty Officers stood had their duties outside of the Main Engine Room in Central Control Station or CCS.

For the main Engine Room watch, two sailors were on duty, a non-commissioned Petty Officer and a Fireman.

Fireman duties while at sea were to stand Sound & Security Watch; making rounds of the entire length of the 563 foot vessel. A Fireman was also on watch to assist the NCO with maintenance or repairs of any machinery that required such.

I carried a duty belt, flashlight, clipboard with a log sheet and pencil, and a sounding tape on a reel. Taking soundings on a ship was important.

While making rounds we were to look for anything amiss, check for fire safety issues, faulty machinery, light bulbs that need replacement, and anything else out of the ordinary. I was to report to the Petty Officer of the Watch anything that I found that needed attention. I was to immediately sound the alarm in case of a dire emergency such as fire or flooding.

Time passed. Life seemed grand.

I was working and learning all I could about the shipboard Engineering Department and the way of a ship in general. I had settled into a pretty good routine.

When I had liberty call and time to venture off the ship and into Charleston, Bruce and I found a few of the local nightclubs.

One of the small clubs that I remember was called "Some Place Else," and it was located within walking distance outside one of the gates to the Naval Station on Meeting Street. The club was always full, and the dance floor always seemed to be moving from the weight of patrons who danced the night away.

There were times when I would venture out alone and find a movie or do some shopping. I still held my penchant for reading. Not that I was an exceptional reader. Through trial and error, with the help of a good dictionary, I developed as a better reader as time went on.

This meant reading pulp fiction and short stories that seemed to better hold my attention span. Now that I had a little pocket money to spend, I would buy magazines and periodicals that I could not readily afford as a bum kid on the street.

Reading through U.S. Navy technical manuals on engines and other machinery came next. I did not understand much of what I attempted to read. But with a patient eye I was able to grasp and make heads and tails of some of what I was reading in this text manuals.

Moving at a slow pace, I was learning a little bit more each day in the engineering department on the 'Moose. There a couple of older sailors, guys who had been to U.S. Navy A Schools and C Schools, as they were called, who taught me the hands on, on-the-job-training (OJT) method of being a mechanic or Engineman.

This was my calling. I truly enjoyed working in the engineering department. Getting greasy and dirty as a "snipe" suited me just fine. I carried a wrench and a flashlight. I loved to pull machinery apart with tools and brawn - and put the pieces back together again.

Communicating with my family, writing letters, making long distance telephone calls, I learned that a few of my friends were taking the wrong path in their young lives. I was not unmindful that I could have taken the same turn.

I learned news that the crew from Rhode Island Avenue NE were all starting to use narcotics with more frequency. I thought about these things for a minute. Rhode Island Avenue seemed like a million miles away. No, I didn't miss any of what was going on there. But I tried to understand and get an idea of what was going on.

My life had changed. The streets of D.C. were behind me now. I wanted to look forward. I was determined to make choices that were commensurate with developing a positive future for myself, and maybe then I could reach back and help bring those close to me along. My concern for family and close friends weighed heavy inside my head.

Word was passed around that the 'Moose would be going to see again real soon. We took on stores, which meant we loaded ample quantities of food and supplies and ammunition.

We were making quick preparations to sail for the shipyard in Pascagoula for some immediate upgrading of weapon systems and refits.

Our schedule was to call at Port Everglades again, which was Fort Lauderdale, before making our run into Pascagoula. Upon leaving Mississippi, the ship would head south through the Gulf of Mexico, into the Caribbean Sea, taking the crew into Guantanamo Bay, Cuba and onto to Charlotte Amalie again. Sounded like great news to Bruce and myself.

Our second visit to Pascagoula allowed us an opportunity to take a better look at the town. A year had passed, and we were becoming more seasoned. Bruce and I found the local night spots, a couple of small juke joints, but the best venue for nightclub like scenes was "The Elks Club" that was in adjacent town of Moss Point, Mississippi.

One weekend we rented a vehicle and made a drive into New Orleans to find Bourbon Street and patronize "the action" that was there.

We were having the time of our lives. I was just nineteen years old, but I was having some great experiences through the course of my travels. The scenes were bright and without any schism that would be cause for alarm. As good as its reputation, New Orleans was a fantastic town to party in.

Leaving Pascagoula, the ship sailed through the Gulf of Mexico and into the Caribbean Sea for Guantanamo Bay, Cuba (again). The U.S. Naval Station in Cuba was called "Git-Mo" and that wasn't very exciting. At Git-Mo Bruce and I found the package store and shared a bottle of whiskey. There wasn't much to do. Weeks went by.

We had quite a few shipboard "battle station" drills on the ship. My battle station was Repair 5, and my duties were to be "number 2 man on number 2 hose." Number 2 hose was a hose that sprayed Aqueous Film Fire Fighting agent or AFFF ("A-triple F") on flammable liquid fires (primarily in the Engineering Spaces).

Completing Sea Trials and ship board drills at Guantanamo Bay, the ship sailed back into the Caribbean and made a direct jaunt for the Virgin Islands. The ship sailed high on bright blue water. The sun burned a great beacon of heat in the sky.

We were sailors and we were going to "paint the town" in Charlotte Amalie when we hit the beach. Seemed like every group of guys that hung out together (on the ship) had their plans and expectations.

 On my 19th birthday, during the first week of August 1979, I was hazed by my shipmates, the sailors in M-Division. It was all in fun. The guys sang "Happy Birthday", I was held down and covered with thick gray grease from head to toe. Grease was smeared all over my body. I took all in stride.

Thus, was the life of a sailor.

CHAPTER FOUR

Not long after my nineteenth birthday on the 'Moose, I was going about my watch standing duties, the "Sound & Security Watch," and as I made my rounds I had some confrontation with a young white sailor about my age. He was from another ship but temporarily assigned to the 'Moose.

This sailor was a Fireman. Cannot recall his name. But he was the same rank and rate as myself. I cannot remember what upset this guy, but for some reason, he became infuriated and expressing his emotions he loudly cried out to me, "You nigger! You nigger!"

I was blind-sided. Out of the blue.

But there it was. A sharp word. An angry word. Cutting with hostility. We clashed and fought with our fists. He swung his fists, and I swung my fists. I was called off by a 2nd Class Petty Officer, who said, "Greg, don't hit him again! Don't hit him again!"

Both his eyes were blackened when I stopped punching.

This attack, yielding the weight of racism, came from out of nowhere. I was nineteen years old. I was probably more naive to this kind of situation than I can recall, and I was only prepared to respond with my fists.

Right away I knew that I had responded in the wrong manner. The fight was a big mistake on my part. But this was what I knew. An unjaded memory rang inside my head. It rang like a bell. And just like that, I was on my feet and answering that bell. Fighting.

A number of other sailors aboard the 'Moose, white and black, heard about the incident.

I was the only black guy in my division, M-Division, but I was asked my side of the story by all the guys I worked with; each one of them listening to my side of the story. Lending an ear of support was better than nothing. I was advised to "cool off" and stay away from the sailor who I had fought with.

None of them were critical of me, though it was obvious that I had handled the situation in the wrong way. And I should have handled it differently. For the most part they felt that this other kid was wrong (he was a sailor from another ship - not assigned to our ship).

A few of the guys suggested to me that I should have come to them. The suggestion was, "Next time just tell the Senior Chief, Greg," and I should have kept this as a forethought.

Neither of us, the kid who called me out of my name nor myself, got into trouble for this fight. But the word still went around, and there were looks and questions for other crew members.

I knew that I had made a bad choice to fight, and I didn't feel good about any of it.

We called at port in Charlotte Amalie. Bruce and I went ashore early in the afternoon to check out the island.

We did some shopping, picking up a few small things, a small piece of gold jewelry, a souvenir tee shirt, and looked around. and took in the day time sights. It was hot, and the sun felt good on my face.

It was late in the afternoon when we returned to the ship, we were planning to rest up, and then find "the action" on the island later that night.

I was standing at my locker putting away the items that I had purchased ashore. Suddenly, maybe fifteen or more drunken white sailors broke in on me. None of these sailors were from my division (M- Division).

They were Hull Technicians or Electricians. Second Class Petty Officer Jim Murdock was their leader, "There he is, there's the bad nigger, right there!" he shouted.

This was the belligerent mob that I had expected in some areas of Alabama or Mississippi. But here it was now on a United States Navy ship.

I turned to face them. A space of maybe 20 feet separated us. They were all drunk, a few of them too drunk to stand straight, so drunk that they staggered around for something hold on to.

Jim Murdock was reputed to be a tough guy. But I saw him as a bully; large built and intimidating to some. I had never talked to him. Never worked with him. He wasn't in my division.

"Yeah! Yeah, that's him, Jimmy!" another drunk voice chimed in, encouraging Murdock.

Heeding the encouragement, Murdock bellowed, "Bad ass nigger, c'mon! C'mon, nigger!" spittle dribbled from his twisted back lips as he went on, "you supposed to be a bad nigger, c'mon! C'mon and give me two black eyes! Murdock was shouting at the top of his voice now, "Give me two black eyes if you so bad!"

I held my ground. I stood straight and looked them all in the face. I was ready to defend myself.

One of them, an Electrician named Dolphinson, said, "He isn't that bad is he Jimmy?"

Murdock screamed, "Ain't no bad niggers! A nigger is the filthiest piece of dirt that ever walked the face of the earth!" Another voice, "He don't look so bad, Jimmy, not now."

Murdock kept it up, "C'mon, nigger. C'mon, nigger boy, c'mon nigger an' give me two black eyes," Murdock begged me to fight him. But there were too many of them. They were drunk and mindless. I was shocked. I felt betrayed.

If I met the challenge they would have beaten me to death. That was my exact feeling. But I stood still and held my ground. Held my ground out of fear rather than courage.

The word "nigger" resonated throughout the berthing compartment. It was hostile, and it was frightening. A big load of weight for a nineteen-year kid to take in.

These were my shipmates. Plank Owners like myself. The shock of the entire episode left me rooted where I stood. Unable to move.

After a minute or two, could have been longer, Murdock grew tired of calling me a "nigger" and staggered to his rack (bed) and collapsed to sleep it off. All his friends dispersed and went their own way. Though no one had touched me, I felt a great sense of being pushed and punched.

I wasn't looking for trouble. Up until now all I knew was that the word "nigger" was the word of hate that some white people used to dehumanize black people.

It was a reality that black people used this word themselves, seemingly to take verbal punches at each other. It was a paradox. Not something clearly understood. I had heard the word thrown in anger from all sides, it was damaging, and it was a threat anytime it came from an angry mouth; white or black. Sometimes it was a dangerous threat.

I did not blame white people, I did not blame the government, and the white guys that I worked with were decent guys and treated me as a fellow sailor, if not as a friend. Blaming no one, I brooded, grew sullen, and blamed myself for not being in control of my own behavior. I didn't have an answer.

If I were not a fighter, it is likely my self-control would've been a lot better than it was. Nevertheless, my attitude began to change.

After the incident with Murdock and his guys I was not the same. I frowned each time I saw one of them. I tried to stay focused on my duties. But I was slipping into a depression of sorts. Bad ideas and worse feelings grew inside of me. Discord developed in my head. And slowly my attitude soured.

The 'Moose was at sea again and sailing for the shipyard in Pascagoula. Everyone, from the bridge to the bilge, was busy standing their watches, eating, sleeping, and resting up from the wild partying that had taken place in Saint Thomas.

Daniels and I were alone one day in the berthing compartment.

He was one of the drunken sailors that had joined Murdock during his verbal assault and racist reproach. Our dislike for each other was mutual. Daniels was a bigot, and I was offended.

Sober now, Daniels gave me an arrogant and knowing look, reminding me that he supported racism, wanting me to know that he hated me because I was black – and without words we started fighting. Just like that. Swinging our fists at each other. He was raging in anger. Likewise, I was furious. Daniels punched hard, and I punched hard. It was an all out brawl.

Out punching him, he screamed when my fists began to rain down on his head and face. He could not keep up, and his head and face took the punches. I beat him with so many blows that I feared reprisal from the Master at Arms.

I threw a very hard punch, knocking him sideways up against a bulkhead (wall), he grabbed me and tried to wrestle, tried to overpower me. He was strong willed.

Shifting my weight, with speed and agility, I took his head in my hands and pounded his head against the bulkhead. I beat his head several times against the bulkhead.

Suddenly, a Second Class Petty Officer came into the berthing compartment, saw us fighting, and barked very, very loudly, "Break it up! Break it up!"

Murdock was next. I knew his watch schedule, as all watch schedules were posted on a bulletin board, and I was ready for him.

He was not a small man. He stood over six feet tall, carried over 200 pounds. But it didn't matter. I was fired up on adrenaline. Fighting didn't matter to me. I had fought several bullies before on the streets of Washington, D.C.

Alone, I waited in the main passageway on the starboard side inside this small alcove in the bulkhead, waited for him to pass by on his way to his watch. He would be sober now. It would be just him and myself. I would find out how bad he really was. I wanted to see if he would call me out with angry names again.

Murdock came along the passageway, and I stepped from the alcove with my fists clenched tight. My face was twisted into the craziest grimace that I could contort. I was ready to battle. One on one, I was not intimidated by this guy at all. None of this is to say that I could have beaten Murdock. I was just plain angry.

Murdock slowed down and was hesitant when he saw me. I was fired up on adrenaline.

As he cautiously approached I stared in in the eye with a dare, quickly he lowered his head, bowed out, and quickly walked past me. If he had given the slightest indication that he would fight me I was set to jump on him with as many lefts and rights as I could throw. I was afraid, but I was fired up.

Without the courage of liquor and his friends backing him up he was not so bad. He didn't look at me or acknowledge me. He walked past me. (in retrospect, this was a good thing.)

"Punk ass," Loud enough to be heard, were the only words my anger allowed.

Very likely, Murdock was smart and wanted no trouble, especially now that he was sober; and maybe he would have beaten me senseless. I had not regarded him as a pushover. Without question, he appeared capable of defending himself and fighting well. But I was emotion driven and didn't care.

After these confrontations my attitude began to change even more. Increasingly, I was cautious around every antagonizing face that had stood with Murdock and Daniels when they had verbally assaulted me with threats of violence.

Suspicion and distrust of others began to affect me. A handful of African-American sailors presented themselves as trouble makers as well. A few black crew members spoke as though they were racists in their own right; some who talked tough about inflicting pain or hurt upon white sailors.

One of these guys, black kid from Philadelphia, was breaking into lockers of his white shipmates and stealing their money and other valuables. Because these victims of his larceny were white guys he fostered some idea in his head that it was okay to steal their money and property.

The picture he painted was smeared. I saw this black kid as being just as much as bigot as any bigot, and on top of that he was stealing. A black bigot and thief.

The 'Moose was docked in the shipyard in Pascagoula and the crew had settled into a routine. The local nightclubs and juke joints were revisited.

Meeting women and getting drunk was still a big deal. Some of the sailors were known for being boisterous and rowdy. There were fights from time to time.

We had a sailor, this big guy from Ohio, a black sailor, who had had been in the Army and served in Vietnam before crossing over into the Navy.

Some of the crew considered him to be a bad ass. The fact that he had been on the ground in Vietnam and seen combat bolstered his image of being a bad ass. His size alone was intimidating. Compared to the skinny recruits and apprentices, such as myself, his hulking appearance was like that of a heavyweight champion. His name was Fenetton.

One evening, while sitting on the mess decks, I ran into a confrontation with the "big guy" from Ohio.

I was eating chow when he sat directly across from me at a table and started, "You don't eat no pork, do you, Greg?" His tray of food was running over the side with pork chops that were glistening with grease. I had no meat on my tray at all. He snickered and giggled.

"No, man, I don't eat pork. I don't eat much meat." I answered., thinking he only wanted to be friendly and conversational.

He grinned, "Oh, you don't eat pork, huh? Oh, you don't eat meat at all, do you?" I sensed the bully rising in him.

I was calm about it, "Be cool, man. I just don't eat a lot of meats." I was hoping he would settle down and eat his food in peace. But he didn't like my response.

"You bad, isn't you, Greg? You one of them bad dudes from D.C., isn't you?" his voice was not friendly nor pleasant.

"Man, I'm just trying to eat," I answered.

"But you one of them bad dudes, aren't you? And you don't eat no pork, do you, Greg?" he said in an agitated voice. He was clearly trying to start something.

Little doubt, he had gotten wind of the fight I had with the white sailor, the one with the two black eyes, and now he was pressing me, trying to see how far he could push me.

"Alright, you punk," I was hot now, "you want a piece of me, bring your punk ass up to the helo-hangar," and with that I took my tray to the scullery and headed two decks up to the helo-hangar. I don't know what had gotten into me. But I was ready to fight.

Inside the "helo-hangar" was where two anti-submarine warfare helicopters were kept (when they were on board), and there was a basketball court there – and we would go there and settle beefs or disagreements with our fists.

When sailors on the ship had a fist fight in the helo-hangar it was an unwritten rule that when they left the helo-hangar the beef would be over and done with. Nothing more would be said.

Bruce and about six more sailors (who had overheard my challenge) hurriedly followed Fenetton as he stormed his way in anger to the helo-hangar.

Bruce later told me that they all thought I was done for a severe beating. Fenetton had been to Vietnam and seen action. Fenetton was an intimidating and aggressive figure. If he wasn't bad, he sure put on a good front. Just his size and age made him bad.

As soon as Fenetton appeared through the hatch leading into the helo-hangar I hit him in his broad face with a four-piece combination. He grinned like a maniac, never stopping his stride as he came through the hatch.

"Oh, you serious ain't you? You think you bad for real, huh?" he chimed in a sing-song like voice. "I'm gonna kill you, I'm gonna kill you, you bad ass 'fucka." He never stopped grinning as he spoke. His grin slobbered over.

His voice turned stupid, nearly incoherent as he mouthed, "C'mon, c'mon, c'mon," as we circled each other.

I skipped my 150 pounds to my toes, dancing in a circle, I popped off another four-piece combination into his face, splitting his lips as my hard fists found their mark.

Fenetton growled and lunged at me. I side stepped him, hitting him with a volley of uppercuts from both hands, ripping open the soft flesh around his eyes, blood ran down his face.

Literally, he roared as though he were insane and charged me. I skipped sideways, again, and hit him four more times about his thick skull.

He was cursing and crying out. Suddenly his fists flurried with energy. I lost count of his punches. And then he grabbed me. Lifting me from my feet he slammed me to the cold steel deck of the helo-hangar and pinned me down.

He had me now. I was trapped. He punched blow after blow with his fist, beating my head and face. Wasn't much I could do. Twisting from side to side I dodged some of his thudding punches.

He screamed, "I'm gonna kill you for this! I'm gonna kill you for this!" he was crying tears of anger as he swore to take my life. "I'm gonna kill you!"

Fenetton used his ham-like forearms like they were heavy wood clubs, beating my face, beating my neck, pummeling me hard. Each punch rattled my senses.

I yelled, "Get off me and fight!" at the top of my voice.

More brutal punches, thundering blows rained down on my head and face. I was being beaten senseless. Each punch jarred my mind like a shaky flash of light.

A fast thought blurred my mind that he might indeed kill me (as he swore to do).

And then things happened real fast. Quickly, I twisted half-way from beneath him and with all my might I threw a punch, a straight right hand. My fist caught him on the chin, snapping his huge face backward.

It was the punch that I needed. Fenetton was rocked on his heels from this hard blow to his face. This was my chance.

Scrambling to my feet, I caught him with another punch, a strong left hook, and he reeled back on his heels again; his eyes stunned wide. He stumbled and fell backwards and hard toward the steel girders of the bulkhead.

Balanced on my feet now, I drove a stiff right hand into his large face.

I saw, and heard, the back of his head clang and reverberate against a steel girder. His head jerked forward. And then I was on him – with my feet.

I kicked him in the head and face. I kicked him until I kicked the heel of my left shoe off. His face was torn and bleeding from the strong kicks. It was ugly.

Fenetton had bullied me. He had asked for it.

With the heel of my shoe kicked off, I slowed down, and I saw that his face was a mass of red jelly. Strips of torn flesh hung loose from over the top of his eyes. One of his lips was badly torn and dripping blood. Teeth were missing from his mouth.

I turned to walk away. I thought Fenetton was finished.

But I was wrong. He wasn't giving up. He staggered up to his feet, grabbed a handful of heavy chains, and whirling them wildly above his head he tried to rush over and hit me with the swinging chains. The chains would have caused a severe injury.

Tottering on weakened legs, he yelled, "I'm gonna kill you for this! I'm gonna kill you for this! I will kill you!" he was deranged and out of his mind with anger.

Fear welled inside me. Again, I thought that he would kill me. I had to do something real fast. My eyes looked fast for something to match against his weapon of chains.

I grabbed a large, brown colored glass bottle and threw it hard as I could. It was a medicine bottle. It hit him in the face and burst into broken pieces, pills inside the bottle scattered.

He screamed. He went down hard. He kicked. He howled. He had lost his mind. But he stayed down.

Suddenly there was a scary pall over the scene. The sailors watching the fight gave us way. My face and torso were bloody, and my knuckles were bloody and raw. This was the worst fight that I had been in since childhood.

It was a terrible fight. I was a mess with my blood and his blood. One of the worst fights in my life. I struggled to stand straight. Staggering on my feet, I tried to re-gain my composure, trying to stand upright, trying to get my bearings. I felt sick inside.

A young shipmate, Marcus Wilson ran over to me and said in a loud voice, "Goddamn, man, where you learn to fight like that? Damn, you a street fighter, Greg! You a street fighter, Greg!""

His words grabbed me and made me look at him. His words made my eyes open wide. It was almost as though a secret of mine had been uncovered.

The tough times from my past had been concealed. I was beaten up on school yards. I was not always able to fend for myself. In a flash, I had a terrible recollection of terrible days.

Days when my legs were not sturdy. I remembered being accosted and assailed. I thought about how I wanted to fight back. But I remembered how weak and feeble I had been, and how I had not been strong enough to resist any attack.

Now, here I was, some years later in life, having a shipmate exclaim in astonishment, "You a street fighter, Greg! You a street fighter!"

Joining the Navy had provided me a way to put a lock on the door to an unpleasant past. Suddenly, being referred to as a "street fighter" had tripped the lock on this door. Unwittingly, the door swung wide open.

Manic ideas tormented me. I felt cornered. I had to protect myself.

Throwing up my hands, pounding my feet hard against the deck, I stormed away. These were unsettling moments. I found a secluded area on the deck of the ship and I cried for a long time.

I had fought and beaten Fenetton and kicked him in the face. I had scraped and beaten Daniels, beaten his head against a steel bulkhead. And I had accosted and challenged Murdock.

Yet, there was no telling if these guys would get drunk again and try to jump me. Maybe they would seek revenge. No way could I defend myself against a mob of drunken full-grown men. Fenetton had very likely killed people before while in Vietnam. Any one of these guys could easily harm me. A knife in the back was all it would take. It would be foolish to take such a chance.

I made up my mind to get a pistol.

In the following days, verbal exchanges with others became short. To say that I "carried a chip on my shoulder" was a mild way to put this into perspective.

A simmering attitude grew inside of me. It was a bad attitude. Should anyone add fuel to the fire, my bad attitude would burst into a definitive expression of violence.

This would have been the best moment for me to go to someone for help. But I didn't. Too many bad emotions welled within. The recent fighting had opened an old box of bad times.

A distrust of those around me, black people and white people, began to develop. I didn't care what their skin color was. My attitude just took a bad turn and went sour. Each day I grew sullen. Each day I grew worse. I turned away from everyone.

I had great questions inside of myself, and those questions were interchangeable over the course of my life, 'What could I possibly do to protect myself? What could I do to make certain that I would live my life unmolested by others?'

I wanted to turn to someone for help. I worked with a group of engineers that would have helped me. No doubt about that.

Observing my behavior, sailors from my division, M-Division, asked me if I was "okay" or if I needed to talk. But I was young and inexperienced. I had no social skills for "heart to heart" talks. I was full of wild ideas. Too many wild ideas.

The thought of turning to someone for help came into my head – and went out the other side of my head like a streak of lightening. I didn't want any of this. I was too young to think straight, it felt like something was pulling me away from what I wanted; and I was making wrong choices.

I was a sailor. I hoped for a career in the U.S. Navy. Such a life would be full of all the great things that I had imagined for myself as a kid. But now things were going wrong.

The romance of being a sailor and plying the trades across the deep blue sea was fading away.

CHAPTER FIVE

It was an Iver Johnson .22 magnum revolver.

Blue steel. Six inch barrel. Wood grips. It held nine rounds. Holding the weapon in my hand I wondered if anyone had ever been shot with this gun. I was back on the school yard. Standing alone. But with a gun this time.

Old memories of my experience with firearms surfaced. As I held the .22 magnum revolver, I remembered when I saw someone shoot a weapon for the first time. It was a rifle.

Mama was renting rooms in the rowhouse where we lived and one of the boarders, Mr. Jesse, skipped out and did not pay his rent for a couple of weeks. Mama held on to his belongings and clothes.

Drunk on a Friday evening, Mr. Jesse showed up and demanded his property. Mama refused to comply. Mr. Jesse left and returned minutes later with the rifle.

Mama was standing at the top of the second floor landing in the house. She was angry. There was a commotion. I was a toddler, and I came rushing out and grabbed Mama by one of her legs – just then, Mr. Jesse, standing in the foyer of the house, pointed the rifle high and fired a shot.

The shot went into the ceiling. With great commotion, my father and my cousin Raymond arrived on foot, accosted Mr. Jesse, wrested the rifle from his hands, and beat him from the house and away from 5th Street.

I never saw Mr. Jesse again. And I never knew what they did with the rifle.

Loud cracking sounds of gunfire was always the signal to run. And, again, I ran sometimes. Fear was real. Being able to run fast was a survival tactic.

I remembered the first time I actually witnessed someone get shot with a firearm. I was twelve years old.

It was my uncle Melvin who had been shot.

The shots had been loud and startling. Up close. Very frightening. With amazing speed, the assailant had run off in a streaking blur and vanished down the street. I ran, too. I was twelve years old.

Melvin had been fist fighting someone, a stranger, and the stranger pulled a dagger and stabbed Melvin in the eye, and in a flash a relative of the stranger had rushed forward and fired the three rounds.

He was wounded twice. Once in the right arm. Once in the upper right shoulder. Another shot went wild and missed him. I heard the erratic shot pass in front of me. BANG! BANG! BANG!

After that episode I saw people shot with handguns at point blank range. I saw stabbings. Once I witnessed a man hit in the forehead with a claw hammer.

Coincidence would have it that Melvin and I would experience another fear together.

When I was sixteen years old I suffered a gunshot. But I did not hear any report from the weapon. I heard no bang. Likely it was the confusion and shock of the moment.

I had been running down a sidewalk, I crossed over into a parking lot, and I was hit by a car. Or so I believed. No cars were running.

All the cars had been parked.

It was a stray bullet. It had hit me soundly in my upper right leg. There was a gaping hole and a lot of blood.

I was knocked down flat by the force of the bullet. Picking myself up, I tried to run again. But something was wrong.

I ripped open my jeans and there was blood. I stopped and tore the hole in my jeans apart to see better, and there was a gaping hole. Blood poured from the wound. The wound was nauseating. I was dizzy. In my shock I stammered and swore that I had been hit by a car.

Friends saw all the blood pouring from the wound and carried me to the apartment where my mother lived.

Melvin was there. He put a belt tightly around my upper leg, making a tourniquet, and called an ambulance. I swore to everyone, to Melvin, to doctors, and to my parents, "I got hit by a car."

I remember Melvin asking, "Who did this to you? Tell me who did this to you?"

In the hospital, my mother said in a low voice, "You didn't get hit by a car. Tell me what happened?"

The shock of it all overwhelmed my reason and understanding. I left the hospital and went home telling everyone, "I got hit by a car." No one, not even my mother, responded to this anymore.

Likely, everyone, family and friends, considered me out of touch with reality.

No cars were moving on the street. All the cars had been parked. How could I get hit by a parked car?

The trauma of this incident would quietly haunt me for the balance of my life. Sometimes I still believe, "I got hit by a car."

But I was on a ship now. If I shot someone, where would I run to? What street could I take to make good an escape? There were no streets here. Holding the weapon in hand I felt the fear again.

The same fear I had felt at age twelve when my uncle Melvin had been shot. Melvin was probably scared too. Just as I had been scared when I had been shot at age sixteen by that stray bullet in the dark.

I simply did not have the communication skills to address the problems I faced. Toying with a firearm was more than reckless, it was dangerous.

At this time and place in my life, a response with violence, or the threat of violence, was the way I dealt with problems. It was fixed in my mind that the next person, white or black, big or small, that attacked me or attempted to bully me was going to be in for a big surprise.

Not just a "street fighter" anymore, I was now a street kid, and I was regressing, rushing headlong on a path to self-destruction.

My feet felt heavy. I was caught in the thick mire of indecision. Strong and angry ideas of how to "fight back" took hold [of me] from the inside out.

Jeepers was from Delaware. He was a young black kid about my age. He was also known to be one of the thieves on the ship (He had been caught a few times breaking into personal lockers and stealing cash and jewelry).

No one really trusted him because he was known to steal from his shipmates.

Anyway, thinking that he was, at the very least street wise and a stand up dude, I showed Jeepers the revolver as I wrapped it in plastic and stashed it inside a box of laundry detergent.

Within an hour the Master at Arms Chief Petty Officer accompanied by five other Chief Petty Officers were standing at my rack, demanding the I open all my personal lockers.

I opened my lockers and the Master at Arms went directly to the laundry detergent box dumped out the contents - and found the revolver. I was busted. Jeepers was not only a thief he was also a rat. He had become a well-groomed snitch on the ship. Jeepers had ratted me out inside of an hour.

The world around me began to collapse.

I volunteered and joined the United States Navy in search of a way of life that was positive and commensurate with ideals of impartiality and fair play. Up until this point I was holding up my part of the enlistment agreement. But getting caught with a cheap pistol was bad news.

Guileless as I was, I could not see where my decisions were taking me, but beyond all doubt I was making the wrong decisions. I was making the wrong choices fast.

On my quarterly evaluations I was scoring 3.4 and 3.6 out of a possible 4.0 in the areas relevant to my rank and rating. I was a good sailor. But now with this negative atmosphere arising all my hard work was being threatened.

Being a sailor was very important to me. The bad decisions were overwhelming me.

My sleep was filled with bad dreams. I lost my appetite. I thought about drinking alcohol. I asked around about pills. I consumed whatever I could get my hands on. When my mind was drugged I lapsed into unconsciousness and slept heavily.

A day or so later, the ship set sail for Charleston, with ports of call in the Virgin Islands and Puerto Rico where there would be liberty call. I fixed my mind to get a bottle of liquor and to find some reefer and smoke it.

When the word went around the ship that I, Fireman Greg White, had been caught with a revolver onboard - nearly everyone shied away from me. Sailors outside of my division stood clear when I walked anywhere on the ship.

Seckinger and Dutch and Don Brown and others in my division treated me no different, we were "snipes" and friends; but no doubt they assumed that I was crazy. Bruce and Rick remained my friends.

I sucked it up, knowing that when we sailed into port at the U.S. Naval Station, Charleston, South Carolina, I was going to be subjected to disciplinary action in accordance with the Uniform Code of Military Justice, commonly known as the "U.C.M.J."

My young life took a real bad turn.

Under the guidelines of the U.C.M.J. I was subjected to nonjudicial punishment of 30 days of hard labor in the newly established U.S. Naval Correctional Custody Unit, referred to as "C.C.U.", for illegally possessing the .22 magnum revolver and bringing it aboard the ship.

C.C.U. was an innovative disciplinary concept, an alternative to "the brig" or a U.S. Naval Prison. C.C.U. was a lot like boot camp with a great deal of punishment.

Ideologies of hard labor and military infantry drill was the order of the day. The rules were simple enough: you were expected to keep your mouth shut and you were expected to work. Hard labor. Six days a week.

There were stories that C.C.U. had been the cause of death for at least two sailors. The reputation of C.C.U. was scary. The compound for the barracks was in a far reaching end of the Naval Station, alongside the Cooper River, perched beneath heavy foliage on a dirt road that no one traveled.

The Non-Commissioned Officer in Charge, the warden, of CCU in Charleston was Senior Chief Petty Officer Tannhauser, "Gentle Ben" he was called (after the bear in the TV show).

He was one of the few remaining sailors from the ranks of the Underwater Demolition Team (UDT), who were, during this time (1979), known as UDT/Seals. Senior Chief had been in the U.S. Navy for well over twenty years.

There were three levels of prisoners. Level One. Level Two. Level Three. Talking was forbidden for Level One prisoners. Level Two prisoners could talk to each other during smoke breaks. Level Three prisoners could talk to other Level Three prisoners at any given time.

The guards were all First Class Petty Officers or Platoon Sergeants in the U.S. Marine Corps. These sailors and marines were a strict crew of guys.

Military drill and discipline was their way. As for the prisoners, there were 25 to 30 sailors sent to CCU at a time. The stay at CCU was to be for 30 days. We were a ragtag crew of wayward young sailors.

We were roused from our racks every morning at 4:30am. No exceptions. In military formation we marched to breakfast.

Afterwards, we changed into UDT hot pants, tee shirts, and boondockers, formed ranks of three abreast - and we ran for five miles in this formation alongside the Cooper River. As we ran, with the Senior Chief leading the way and calling cadence, above our heads the hot July sun was burning away.

Any excess fat that was on my 150 pound frame melted away. We did this six days a week.

After our morning run, we showered, dressed in working uniforms, fell back outside the barracks in formation, and marched off into the heavily wooded area close to the river - and set to chopping down trees (with axes or a two-saw) and clearing the way for some open ground.

Other work details included digging ditches along the dirt and gravel road, wielding sledge hammers to bust large rocks and stones, and working on a large piece of asphalt with pneumatic powered jack-hammers.

Days and nights in C.C.U. were long and dark. The routine never wavered. Marching to the galley. Standing for inspection.

Running five miles six days each week. Marching into the forest to chop down trees, or to the rock pile to swing a sledge hammer.

Senior Chief was a hard nose sailor. I have no doubt that he was capable of violence. But he was fair and a straight shooter. He was always seemed calm and in control of himself.

Military marching drill was a mainstay, and there were visits to the shooting range at the Naval Station. We were instructed and given an opportunity to qualify for ribbons with pistols at the range.

When my turn to shoot came up, to my surprise and satisfaction, I scored well and qualified as expert with a pistol. I earned a ribbon. Blue, thin green stripe, with an "E" centered in the middle.

This was a prime chance for me to get myself together. Correct my behavior. I should have made the best of my thirty days of punishment and took a step forward. If I had been smart I would have sucked it all up and found my way back to the 'Moose and resumed my duties as a Fireman.

But I was not smart. I entered C.C.U. with a bad attitude. I was imprisoned, and I resented it. I grew rebellious and made wrong decisions.

They called it "The Quiet Room." It was an empty barren jail cell with a round six inch diameter hole in the concrete deck that was to be used as a toilet. The solid concrete bulkheads

(and the deck) was painted a dark blood red color. Insects scurried across the barren deck. The stink rising from the six inch diameter hole was terrible and stomach wrenching.

When two of the guards put me in there, I was told by one of them to stand at attention with my face in a corner. I did as I was told. Until they left.

Catching me not standing with my face in the corner and laid back on the deck, they were furious and promised retribution. I laughed. What could they do? There were only two of them.

They left. Minutes later when they returned they brought the whole lynch mob. There were at least half-dozen Petty Officers and one Marine, a real "Jar Head" who projected the characteristic image of being a tough guy.

They rushed me. I caught one of them with a straight right hand and he dropped. And then they were all over me.

Punches landed on me from all angles. Fists rocked my skull and bruised my flesh. My teeth wrenched loose and cracked. They beat me mercilessly. I struggled and kicked. My fight was useless.

Two of them grabbed me and pinned me against the bulkhead, while the marine stepped in with a leather encased black jack and smacked lick after lick about my rib cages.

Letting me collapse to the deck, they all began using their boots on me, kicking me from head to toe. I was kicked and beaten into unconsciousness.

When I came around, I was naked.

Tight fitting handcuffs held my arms behind my back, and chain-linked shackles of leg irons were clamped tight around my ankles.

Grit from dirty footprints covered my bare torso. My lips were cracked and split and tasted of dried blood. Painful lumps dotted my skull. My ribs were swollen and bruised with pain. There was dirt all over me where their boots had landed.

Trussed in these chains, I thought I was going to die. It was amazing that no permanent injuries were sustained. Still, I would not have been able to walk away from this mob violence (if there had been an open door).

In fact, I could not stand, and I lay there on the concrete deck in my own filthy blood stains. It had been a nightmarish ordeal. I had been given a beating that I will never forget.

There were other sailors (prisoners) that rebelled in C.C.U. Troy Giles from New York City. Timothy Moss and Carson, both from Detroit. Decker from Rochester, New York, and a couple of others would frequently be place in "The Quiet Room."

However, I believe Carson and myself were kept in "The Quiet Room" more than any others in CCU at that time. We were all beaten. Black sailors and white sailors.

Sleep deprivation was used as punishment in The Quiet Room. Without exception, the lights were kept shining brightly twenty-four hours a day, seven days a week.

When the guards wanted to keep us from sleeping, they would pull a small chair or stool up to the cell bars, sit there with a long broom stick in hand - and poke us to keep us awake if we closed our eyes and dozed off. This would usually be done over the course of a three day minimum. Sleep deprivation is torturous.

Being denied sleep was annoying and unsettling. Mental anguish soon followed, and the discomfort was a maddening experience.

The guards, sailors and marines alike, who subjected us (prisoners) to sleep deprivation did so with the demeanor of a mischievous rascal. Their smirking faces were alert and marred with delight when they used broomsticks to nudge and prod our naked bodies, not allowing us to sleep.

Very likely it was my experience with sleep deprivation that pushed me over the edge. It was an agonizing experience.

Anxiety was fostered deep within and affected my spirit. I lost respect for my captors, and for the authority entrusted in them.

The beatings in the Quiet Room overshadowed any ordinary events, or day to day routines. For example, I cannot recall what the food was like while in the Quiet Room. Meal time meant little when sleep deprivation was being employed. Besides, the meals were little more than cold piles of slop.

With resentment welling inside of myself, I felt badgered and needled. I was pushed hard. Or at least that's what I felt at the time. The experience was nerve-wracking. My judgement was marred. A feeling of agitation made me shake inside. Despair was overwhelming.

I wondered, 'Why is this happening to me?'

I asked myself more questions. I wondered why things had taken such a dramatic turn in my life.

Shortly, no more than two days after being released from the Quiet Room, a confrontation between myself and the guards ensued. One of the guards started in on me (again) and responding in anger I smashed and destroyed a small, four-legged wood table.

Breaking off a table leg from the flat top, I began swinging the makeshift club. I hit two of the guards upside the head with the table leg.

They cried out and ran. I chased them, clubbing the backs of their shoulders, catching one of them with a good lick soundly in the head.

The guards were in a state of confusion now. Never had they imagined that they would one day meet any opposition and answer for the brutality they had inflicted.

I turned over tables and chairs and a small desk. I wrecked a couple of racks (bunk beds).

And then I chased all the guards through the main corridor. I was vengeful. I wanted to bust heads. And I did.

When all the guards were run off, I walked to the lock-up tier on my own, went into one of the "Quiet Rooms" and sat down on the concrete deck.

I resigned to being locked away in this barren place and prepared to face the wrath of the guards when they mustered and came to beat me with their sticks and use their boots on me. Maybe they would use gas. I closed my eyes.

But they did not come. Everything grew quiet.

I clearly heard the Senior Chief shouting from down the tier. He was furious and livid with exasperation, "I want Fireman White out this building! Take him to the brig!" which was the U.S. Naval Correctional Center.

The threat of being sent to the brig was frequently used to control behavior. The brig was supposed to be a bad place, a real jail atmosphere. No one wanted to be there.

Within an hour I was inside a gray U.S. Navy van and being hustled fast to the U.S. Naval brig.

At the brig, The Master Chief, the Duty Warden laughed hard when he was told the story of how I had beaten the C.C.U. guards with a wood table leg.

The guards escorting me didn't like it, but he Master Chief told them that he had no authority to lock me up in the brig (because I had not been sentenced at any court-martial to military prison; there were no orders of confinement.

The Master Chief made some phone calls and learned that my ship, the USS Moosbrugger, was out at sea, taking me to my ship was not an option.

The guards from C.C.U. insisted that the brig take custody of me. The Master Chief told them he would keep me there (until they worked it out). The guards from C.C.U. left me at the brig.

When the guards were gone the Master Chief turned to me and asked, "Are you gonna behave yourself, White?"

"Yes, Master Chief," I answered with respect.

"Well, I'm gonna release you to the Legal Holding Barracks 31 on the base. You'll stay there until your ship comes back to port."

Legal Holding Barracks, better known as Barracks 31, or often just "31", was where U.S. Navy misfits, renegades, dissenters, and other wayward sailors were housed.

Some sailors in Barracks 31 were awaiting their ships to come back to port (as I was), some others were awaiting court-martial, some had recently been released from the Brig or CCU, and some were waiting for orders to be sent to a ship elsewhere in the fleet.

Those awaiting court-martial while housed in 31 were likely to be sent to the brig.

Sailors awaiting court-martial from the brig were likely to be sent to the United States Disciplinary Barracks in Fort Leavenworth, Kansas.

Barracks 31 was the "animal house" of the U.S. Naval Station in Charleston.

From the 4th floor windows of the block long brick building, small clouds of marijuana smoke could be seen drifting out and high into the air.

Illegal drugs flourished freely in Barracks 31. Pills and powders and micro-dots of acid. Nobody cared what the fifty or sixty odd sailors assigned to 31 did inside the fence.

Everyone came and went through Barracks 31 in a free-for-all. I went U.A. my first night there. "Unauthorized Absence." I caught a Trailways bus bound for Washington, D.C. and I went home.

The shock of C.C.U. was overwhelming. I was disillusioned, and I took flight. My decision to cut out was deliberate. I saw a small space of daylight, and I ran.

I carried an overnight bag and a bottle of cheap liquor. I had little doubt that I was making bad decisions. The spirits only made me feel worse, coaxing me into a nauseated slumber.

As the Trailways Bus pushed north from the Carolina's and into Virginia, I curled on the rear seat and contemplated my life, thought about where I was going.

I drank the cheap liquor to numb myself, to lapse into a slumber. As I wanted to make vague the memory of what summed up the balance of my callow ways.

I wanted to push away the thought and the idea of my past. But I couldn't sleep. I had long been told, and reminded with stern convictions, that I was worthless. The memory of these edicts lingered.

An idea came to mind, I would locate the recruiter, the Senior Chief, who had enlisted me into the Navy. Maybe there was some chance he could help me challenge the abuse that I had been subjected to.

It was an idea that I kicked from one corner inside my head to the next corner inside my head. I wanted optimism. I wanted a way to improve my behavior. But I felt overwhelmed.

Looking out the window of the Trailways Bus I could see the reflections of all that I wished to understand.

Where was I going? Where had I come from? What would be waiting for me at the next stop? The road was open. In both directions.

Reassessing myself to gain some control, to foster a good chart and position, I looked back over the short span of my life for a long while. The back seat of the Trailways Bus rumbled and would not settle. The road seemed to wind away forever.

I remember feeling dirty when I stepped off the bus and took to the streets of Washington, D.C. Making a radical decision to go U.A. was wrong. I was still quite young. My mistakes had not accumulated in such a way to be a complete disaster. Amending the damage was possible. I could well have gone to someone for help.

My decisions were all wrong. I was stoking the fire for bigger and bigger trouble. Making matters worse for myself. This was the bane of being young and reckless.

Being U.A. left me very few options. Before long, I was back in the thick of the street, hanging out with petty hustlers, smoking reefer, chasing women, drinking liquor, and gleaning the fast life that I saw all around me. I was going nowhere fast.

Nightlife was large in the city, and 14th Street NW in D.C. was the fast track. Anyone in the life of a hustler or crook knew this was the place to be. It was the area where "the action" could be found.

A couple of weeks went by. I was sleeping on sofas of friends or finding a bed in a flophouse for $10 bucks a night. I told no one that I was U.A. from the military.

I was ready to return to the Naval Station, but I was haunted by what I had experienced in C.C.U., and those shady recollections kept me from turning myself over to the military authorities (who were looking for me). It was a touchy set of circumstances.

And even though I told no one that I had absconded from my military service there were people around me that knew the logic of my circumstance. It was common sense. No one just walked away from the military.

It was 5am in the morning when I heard a stranger's voice call my name. It was a stern voice.
I was still under the influence of alcohol, but I rolled over and the U.S. Armed Forces Police were there. U.S. Army guys. Someone close to me had called them to come and get me. I was devastated.

Placing handcuffs on me, they took me to the Washington Navy Yard in Southeast D.C. and locked me up inside a cold and barren jail cell.

After processing some paperwork, they took me to Bolling Air Force Base to a barracks that was U.S. Navy Annex, where the Navy Honor Guard was housed; the top floor of the building also served as the Legal Holding Barracks.

My ship, the 'Moose, was at sea again and I would have to stay in the barracks in D.C. until orders were processed and forwarded.

CHAPTER SIX

It was hotter than hell in Guantanamo Bay, Cuba.

Back on the 'Moose, Bruce and I reunited and found a fifth of Bacardi 151 proof rum. We took a long walk beneath the Cuban sun, drinking from the bottle, catching up on how things had been in C.C.U. and what was happening on the ship since I had been away.

From Bruce I found out that he and Rick made an attempt to visit me there; they had walked down the dirt road to C.C.U. and knocked on the door and asked to see me. But I had been kicked out by the time they showed up.

We got drunk and staggered around for a long time.

Days later, we were sailing to the Virgin Islands again. Once again, the ship anchored in Saint Thomas-Cruz Bay near Charlotte Amalie. Bruce and I hit the town in stride. We met some brothers who were selling reefer (right out of a bale). I took off my tee shirt and a handful of the wild grown weed was stuffed into the tee shirt.

We found a bottle of rum and walking in Charlotte Amalie we drank and smoked hard. Finding our old haunts and hang out's in Saint Thomas was easy. We went to some nightclub where the women were beautiful, and we stayed there until the place closed in the early hours of the morning.

The word was out. Fireman Gregory White was done. When the ship reached port and was dockside in Charleston, as soon as the gangway was secure, I would immediately be signed off the vessel and shuttled away; sent to the U.S. Naval Correctional Center.

The word going around was that I was a screw up. I was the first Plank Owner to get the shaft, to leave the ships' company in a bad way. The shame of this disgrace was terrible.

A few shipmates bid me goodbye, sailors like Rick, Dutch, Seckinger, Markopolski, Walker, Klump, Depas, Moore, and Farmer, who I had known from Boot Camp, and a few others from other Divisions. Guys like Mike Warren and Mike Morris, and my little brother Denis Taylor.

For me, it was a tough goodbye. This was my first ship. I was a plank owner. A sad feeling overcame me. I was leaving the 'Moose. I had fell short and made great mistakes, yet I steadied myself, and held my sea bag tight by the straps.

The 'Moose was special. She was the first. Leaving the 'Moose was something that hurt me deep inside. I had crawled the length of her from f'oscle to fan tail. Deep inside, I had went into each one of her engineering spaces too many times to count. I had been one of the first "bilge rats" to dive with gusto into the bilge.

Bruce stood close to me and said, "I'll find you." I nodded. We didn't exchange addresses or telephone numbers. None of that. A simple, "I'll find you," and I was gone.

Upon mustering off the USS Moosbrugger DD-980 – standing on the quarterdeck, uncertain of myself, and on nervous legs about what the next turn of events would bring. I wanted to turn and go back. But I could not. Not this time.

I remember the ship's bell ringing loudly. I was surprised and looked up. The startling announcement was loud over the ship's general P.A. system, "Plank Owner, Fireman Apprentice White! Departing!"

I shouldered my sea bag and took a deep breath.

I was taken straight to the brig. Again. And just like before, I had not been sentenced to any time in the brig. There had been no court martial, no legal proceedings at all.

The Duty Warden, the Master Chief (same one as before), tried to explain this to the chasers who took me to the brig. They had no clue what he was talking about. I was left there with the Master Chief.

The Master Chief made telephone calls, telling everyone he spoke with, "I have a sailor here who has not been to any court martial, and I cannot just keep him here because the ship wants me to. He has not been found guilty of anything."

The Master Chief arranged to send me, again, Legal Holding Barracks 31. He admonished me, demanding that I give him my word not to go U.A. again. He told me that I would likely be punished with some time in the brig and then issued orders to report to another ship. But he said, "It's it up you, White."

CHAPTER SEVEN

Back in 31, and I realized once over that this was not the place where the rules and regulations were held in esteem, to say the least. The incentive to be a good sailor was not upheld at the Legal Holding Barracks.

All kinds of characters were in 31. This time around I decided to stay and face my what lay in store for me. I knew that punishment was coming my way. I was prepared. 31 was a continuing serial script straight from "McHale's Navy" and "Hogan's Heroes."

Right away I met Earl Bennett, a black sailor my age from Buffalo, New York. And like myself, he had been subjected to racism aboard the supply ship that he was assigned to. Also, like myself, he had responded with his fists, fighting and taking an "Unauthorized Absence" or going "U.A." as it was commonly referred to.

Within one week we had a crew of new friends.

The crew of sailors that Earl and I met were all about our own age. We were a diverse crew of young guys. We were black, white and Latino. Race didn't matter. Each one of us from a different part of the country. Some of us were from big cities, some were from small towns. Simply put, we were just some kids. I remember these friends well enough.

Camaraderie was unspoken, but it rang true. Cannot forget these guys and the bonds we formed - and "the noise" that we made when we partied as sailors are apt to do.

Oliver, a white sailor from Cleveland. Busted for drugs and going U.A.

Lewis, a black sailor from Chicago. Went U.A.

Superman, a white sailor from Oklahoma. Stole the cash from the safe inside the Disbursing Office on his ship. Because of this bold feat of larceny, he carried a reputation as being a "safe cracker."

Josh, a black sailor from Miami. After getting into fights on his ship, he was awaiting re-assignment to another ship.

Rat, cannot remember his real name, a white sailor from Chicago. Caught dealing drugs on his ship and went U.A.

Curly, a Puerto Rican sailor from Boston. Went U.A.

Gillison, a black sailor from Milwaukee. Went U.A.

Short, a white sailor from the Lower East Side of New York City.

Friendships we forged were genuine. Being a sailor was our adhesive, our binding element.

Earl and I seemed to be the foundation for this group of guys. We were street wise kids. Banded together, we likened ourselves as a real crew of roguish sailors. Easily, I was reminded of the times I had known on "Pirate Lake" as an eleven-year old.

But this time we were young adults. Our choices and antics not without accountability. Wild times, sure. Getting drunk, showing off tattoo's, telling "sea stories" of brothels and fist fights, wrecking bars, and sometimes going to jail. Taking the lumps and the bruises as they came.

On 4th floor of the barracks we would gather, sitting around a table in one of the rooms, a half a pound of marijuana would be dumped on a big table cloth and the smoking would start.

Bottles of whiskey would appear. A plastic sandwich baggy full of illicit pills would come out. A case of beer would be brought in. More whiskey would be opened and poured.

And I remember someone always turning on a "black light," one that would cast an eerie purple color over the entire scene.

An 8-track tape would be jacked into a Panasonic boom box; all volume's turned up, bass and treble adjusted, and the Sly Stone, the Funkadelic, the "Beast of Burden" of the 'Stones, or the "Hollywood Nights" of Bob Seger would take us there. We all agreed that barracks 31 was our very own "Hotel California" and that none of us could ever get out.

Everyone had a story. Some of us shared some of the stories – and some of us blotted out our stories with substance abuse and the dark-gray screen of suppressed emotion.

I was one who opted to blot out my story. Just like in my past, I wanted to forget. Yet, the black light scenes made my memories unforgettable. And when I thought too hard, I smoked more and drank more.

On several occasions, I was given pills and I had no idea what the pills were or what the effects would be. I just took what I could get. My mind would go numb. All my problems seemed to vanish into the warped fog of being on cloud nine.

We would fill the rooms with the fragrance of cheap incense to masque the thick smell of reefer being burned and blown. We partied and shared everything.

One night, Earl and I got our hands on some coarse brown powder with bella donna and sulfur in it. Someone mixed a tablespoon full of this powder in a cupful of purple colored Cool Aide. We drank a cupful. An hour later we were out of our minds. Literally out of our minds.

For a couple of days, I thought I had lost my eyesight. Nearly went blind, and with a mental state that was likened to madness. Earl vanished after drinking the bella donna and sulfur concoction; a toxic mixture of sludge. We looked all over for him. He was nowhere to be found.

Two days later when Earl showed up at our room in the barracks he was naked, save for the bath towel wrapped around his waist. Somehow, he had lost all his clothes while high off the bella donna.

The hallucinating elements in the bella donna had assailed his mental state in a horrific way; and he had ventured nowhere. We realized that he had never left the barracks – and for two days he had been aimlessly walking within the large shower and head (bathroom) areas in the barracks. He was spaced out of his mind.

Oliver was a hippy. He never wore shoes. He wore flip-flops, without socks, and he was well known for having illicit drugs all the time.

When I first met him, I thought Oliver was crazy and tried to shy away from him. He was stoned and had a distant look in his eyes. But we became good friends. He was loyal, and we had a bond of respect for each other's friendship that was genuine and without pretense.

One day I was in my room in the barracks when Oliver came around and told me that he had some hash, asked me if I wanted to get high. In those days drugs were frequently shared among friends. It was all about the party.

"How much you got, man?" I asked.

"I just got a piece from this guy who just got back from Turkey or some place," Oliver with excitement over having scored the piece of hash. A "piece" of has was a block of hash the exact size as a standard pack of cigarettes.

 I said, "C'mon, let's go to the gear locker and smoke it."
We liked smoking in the gear locker because there was so much vice in Barracks 31 [that] the doors had recently been removed from each room. Except for the door on the gear locker.

Oliver and I smoked the entire piece of hash. All of it. It was called "dirty blond Lebanese hash" and it was good stuff.

Our eyeballs were sore when we stumbled from the gear locker, and we were hunched over and laughing aloud. Smoke trailed behind us, and our clothes reeked of the smell of hash.

Not twenty- feet away there were four or five commissioned officers, Lieutenants and Captains, and they saw us. We were busted.

Oliver and I looked at each and broke out laughing louder than before, we had been busted, and there was nothing that could be done. Not really. We were already in Barracks 31 and in hot water.

On another occasion, I was coming out of the front door of Barracks 31 when Oliver drove past in a brand new midnight blue Oldsmobile Cutlass Supreme with a white vinyl top. Seeing me, Oliver came to a stop. Getting into the car I asked, "Where'd you get this, man?"

"From my girlfriend. I'm taking off for Cleveland to see my mom for a couple of days. C'mon, man, ride with me?"

"Let's go," I said. And we were gone. It was late Friday afternoon. We didn't have to muster (be at the barracks) until 8am Monday morning. I got into the passenger seat and we took off.

In his shirt pocket, on a stiff piece of perforated paper about the size of a playing card, Oliver had 40 to 60 hits of "blueline blotter" acid. Blotter acid was liquid LSD sprayed or dipped on perforated paper (formed into small squares). Each square was a "hit" or a "tab". One hit or one tab placed on your tongue would set your mind blazing like roaring fire with remarkable delusions.

Oliver told me that he had taken three or four hits of the acid already, but he wasn't sure. We stopped at a package store and I went in and purchased two cases of beer. Next, we stopped and brought two ounces of reefer.

Out onto the highway we rolled away from Charleston. By the time we reached Columbia, South Carolina, Oliver was so high from the acid, tripping hard, that he could no longer drive the car.

Oliver insisted that the steering wheel on the car was only one inch in diameter - and he was trying to drive by pinching his thumbs and forefingers together, trying to grasp and hold onto what he thought was a very tiny steering wheel. Soon the effects of the LSD overwhelmed Oliver. He laughed and became hysterical.

We had to pull over at a rest stop.

When the acid took effect on my mind I lost track of time and reason. I remember Oliver saying, "Charleston, Charleston, we're in Charleston."

We were in Charleston, West Virginia. Not Charleston, South Carolina. Confused we looked all around. We were still a long way off from Cleveland, and we were tripping out of our minds off the acid.

Looking at each other, we decided to turn back and head for the Naval Station before we wrecked the car or got arrested by the police. This was not a good experience. The interstate highway was not a place to be driving while spaced out on LSD.

Both of Oliver's eyeballs were fireball red. And his hair stood out all over his head in a mad scientist kind of way. Like Oliver, I had lost count of how many hits of the blueline blotter I took. Drinking beer and smoking reefer, we went back to South Carolina. It was a road trip that was "a trip".

One morning after breakfast in Barracks 31 a black sailor named Lewis, a friend of mine from Chicago, part of our crew of friends, came to me and said, "Greg, somebody stole my radio, man. Somebody went into my room and took my box."

I told Lewis that I would keep an eye out for his radio if someone passed by or tried to sell it to me. Guys were famous for stealing petty items and then selling the item cheap. Lewis thanked me and left my room.

Twenty minutes later Lewis returned, announcing that he had good reason to believe that a rowdy crew of white sailor's downstairs on the second floor had his radio. Lewis was a mild mannered kid, laid back, never gave anyone any trouble nor argument. I remember he said, "Greg, they got my box, man."

I raised up, saying, "You sure that it's your box?" I wanted to be certain that when we went to confront these guys that we had just cause.

"Yeah, Greg, they got my box."

"Where you say they at?" I was thinking the situation over quickly. I wanted to help my friend get his radio back.

"They're down on the second floor, it's about eight of them, down there in the supply room. When I ask to see the radio, they were playing they said something smart and started laughing."

"But did you see the box?" I inquired.

No. Not good. But they have it. They are playing music," Lewis was certain they had his radio.

My decision was made, "C'mon, let's go," I said as I laced up my last boot. "When we get down there let me do the talking. If they got that box, they gonna have to give it back." I was ready.

When we got down there we could see the radio, and it was playing music. There was a counter blocking the entrance to the supply room. I hopped over the counter. Lewis followed suit. We stepped into a roomful of sailors who were strangers to us.

I didn't mince words, "Anybody seen a radio, about this big," I motioned with my hands -- and looked at the radio playing music. Not one of the guys said anything. Louder now, "I said, anybody seen a radio down here?"

A couple of the guys shook their heads "no," and I glanced at Lewis. "Is that it, man?"

Lewis shook his head, "No."

We turned to hop back over the counter and leave. And then a loud voice rang out, "We ain't got no goddamn radio belong to you in this here supply de-pot," it was the accent and sound of the deep south, and it was an angry expression that riled my emotions.

Turning to the voice, I asked, "What you say, man?"

"You got a hearing problem, boy? I don't patronize no stinking ass niggah's." He was big and wide. Well over six feet tall. Carrying two-hundred pounds or more.

At the sound of the word "nigger" I jumped forward and hit him with a right cross, splitting the soft meat around his right eyeball. Blood immediately poured from the gash.

He lurched out and tried wrestling me, but my fist were fast, and I beat his face with a lot of punches. He screamed and cursed. Grabbing me, he fell to his knees from the blows from my hard fists.

On his knees he sank his teeth into my left calf, and tried to bite a piece of meat from my leg with his teeth. It was a good bite and it hurt like hell. I kicked him. Once. Twice.

Lewis seized two crutches that were in the supply room and beat the big man upside his head until he let me go.

One of his ears was nearly torn off during the fight. The ear was still attached, but it was a flap of bloody meat. His ear looked horrible.
 Blood was everywhere.

The military authorities hauled the big country sailor to the hospital. Lewis and I were taken into custody.

After questioning us, after learning that word "nigger" was at the root of the fight, the authorities decided they would let Lewis and myself return to Barracks 31 - on the promise that there would be no further aggression on our part. Solemnly, we promised not to fight anymore. We left with every intention to let the matter rest.

Later that day, four of us sitting together at a table in the Mess Hall, which was nearly across the street from Barracks 31. There was Lewis, Gillison, Curly, and myself at a table together. Earl, Oliver, and Superman were sitting at the adjacent table; everyone was talking with excitement about the fight earlier that day.

Getting into fights was commonplace with being a sailor or a marine. Anytime there was a fight there was interest and concern for details. All our friends wanted to know the specifics and "What happened?"

None of us knew who this big country guy was. He presented himself as tough. Not a single person from our circle of friends knew his name nor had anyone seen him around.

One thing was certain, he wasn't a part of our crew, he had made a big mistake and taken a few hard licks, or so we reasoned in our rough and tumble way. We were sailor's. Not saint's. Each one of us hailed from a hard times background. Being sailors befit us like few other vocations could.

Suddenly, without warning nor expectation, the big country guy fell into the mess hall surrounded by a chorus of loud voices, cursing and threatening words.

"Big Country" was accompanied by several of his friends. At least six companions were rallied around "Big Country," his head was swathed in white bandages from the beating he had endured earlier in the day. The Mess Hall was lit up with the shouting of the word "nigger!"

Big Country and his friends were livid and raging with curses, and they wielded and thrust the word as if it were a stiletto or some other sharply penetrating weapon, "nigger!"

My group of friends had to hold me down. Really, we all held each other down. Ushering ourselves from the Mess Hall we made a slow, reluctant retreat to Barracks 31.

None of wanted to get put into the brig. As we went through the mess hall door I distinctly heard, "They got nigger lovers with them! nigger lovers! nigger lovers!"

It was an angry scene. Wanting to avoid more trouble we left the chow hall.

We were upset, but we held ourselves in check. None of us wanted more trouble than we were already in. We went back to Barrack's 31.

White sailors, our friends Oliver, Superman, and Rat, supported us. Talking together we agreed bigotry was "fucked up." We tried to focus our thoughts on getting some cash together for beer and wine. Getting drunk would pass some time and make us feel better. So, we thought.

An hour or so later, were hanging around on the stoop out in front of Barracks 31, drinking beer, some smoking cigarettes. There was Lewis, Gillison, Oliver, Curly, Superman, and myself. We were still talking about the events of the day, some of us commenting on the racism that we had experienced as black sailors in the U.S. Navy.

A pick-up truck sped by. It was them.

"Nigger's go back to Africa!" rang out in a loud voice as the pick-up truck sped away and rounded another corner.

We were alarmed. We glanced at each other. Maybe they had went and gotten a gun or knives.

Looking up, we saw the pick-up truck coming again. His time they were leaning from both sides of the pick-up truck and waving tire irons, chains, and a baseball bat. Boldly, the pick-up truck jumped the curb -- and half a dozen white guys bailed out to do battle.

"Nigger!" was their fight cry. One of them had a confederate flag. They charged our way, screaming.

We met the battle head on.

Bounding rapidly from the stoop of Barracks 31 I grabbed a guy in his collar and hit him with a punch so hard that his shirt tore in my hand and he fell backward.

Lewis was fighting. Curly was fighting. Oliver was punching and kicking. Gillison took a guy by the legs and whirled him around against a tree. Superman was trying to fight (he was drunk).

I caught Big Country, the main antagonist, and I boxed stiff punches all over his head and face with my fists.

The white bandages that he wore from his earlier wounds were ripped away as my fists found their mark with straight right hands and left hooks. He swung wildly, punching with strength, hitting me upside the head.

I turned up the speed of my punches. My hands turned red from the blood. He went down. He fell to his hands and knees in the street. He tried to crawl away, tried to escape the pain.

Leaning in, I threw upper-cuts and bolo punches. With each blow his head would rise and then fall.

The bandages were gone now. I beat them off his head. Blood was all over his face. His injured ear was torn away this time and lay curled in a lump of blood in the street.

I became unhinged. I kicked him. I put my boot deep into the pit of his stomach. Drawing my foot back again, I kicked his rib cage with three solid kicks. I thought about how I had been kicked by that marine corporal in C.C.U.

I heard Lewis scream, "Stop, Greg, you gonna kill him! Stop, Greg, you gonna kill him!"

I came to my senses. I stopped fighting and walked away.

I saw three guys laying in the street. One of them was Big Country. I heard the sirens of the Shore Patrol.

Three other guys jumped back into the pick-up truck and drove away real fast, swerving the vehicle wildly over the curb, and wrecking the pick-up truck as they ran head on into the flag pole in front of barracks 31 and knocked it down.

The sirens of the Shore Patrol were louder now. I fled into the barracks, hurriedly washed my hands and face, went to my room and laid on my rack (bed) and tried to act like nothing was going on.

The Shore Patrol arrived. All sailors who were involved in the fight were rounded up. We all went to the brig. No exceptions. It was a sad day for all of us.

This was a situation that had gotten way out of control. I did not feel good about this fight. I was left with a feeling of disgust, not to mention a massive mess of trouble to wade through – on top of the trouble in my life that was already brewing.

This incident was written about in the local news. It was not uncommon for such news from the U.S. Naval Station to reach the public. This was not the only instance in which news of racial contention, even in small detail, would reached the public ear.

Some weeks prior to our fight there had been a lot of talk around the Naval Station about Keith Hurie.

I had befriended Keith while patronizing the Naval Base NCO Club and the nightclub scene in the area.

Keith, like myself, was a black kid from Washington, D.C. We had met one night at the NCO Club; someone had introduced us as "D.C. guys," and we became acquaintances and later friends.

Keith had recently been in the news for stabbing a young white sailor to death. The news reports had been brief but graphic. It was a story that was spoken of frequently at the Naval Station. Not just gossip, but a serious incident with a grave outcome.

We got the word that Keith was going to stand before a General Court Martial, the most severe court martial proceedings, for the murder of one of his shipmates; a fellow submariner.

It had started over the use of a pool table in the lounge of the barracks where Keith was housed.

Angry, drunken words were exchanged, and emotions flared to a head. The white sailor verbally assailing Keith as "a nigger faggot!" and Keith responding with a pocket knife.

A sailor had been killed. No one took it lightly. This was an extremely unfortunate set of circumstances. The entire affair was talked about a great deal – black sailors and white sailors spoke about the killing.

We were young, yet I thought about Keith and the sailor who had been killed for a long, long time. I considered my own experience with racial prejudice; brooding over the sounds of viciousness when nasty words were spit into someone's face. I had heard such words from black and white people.

Whether the voice came from a black mouth or a white mouth, the hostility of racism was madness.

Murder was a serious crime with serious consequences. My own personal sentiment was that none of this should have happened. None of it.

Earl, Lewis, Oliver, Gillison, and Superman were all standing before a court martial of some type.

Most of the guys were getting 6 months of hard labor in the brig and a discharge that ranged from a Bad Conduct Discharge, the dreaded "BCD", to General Under Honorable Conditions Discharge.

No one wanted a BCD. No one wanted to leave military service with a damaging scar on their record. A BCD was called "bad paper" and could damage a young persons life indefinitely, if not for a lifetime.

Our behavior may have strayed wayward, but we all wanted to be sailors, we all desired to find "our place" in the United States Navy – where we would be accepted and not discriminated against. We were streets kids. Still teenagers. Each one of us. Black and white. What did we know about effective communication?

It was time for me to face another round with the Uniform Code of Military Justice. It was raining when I was shackled and handcuffed and put into a drab gray U.S. Navy van.

I was taken to stand before a Summary Court Martial. There had been a great deal of hell raised in Barracks 31, and the crew of friends that I ran with were responsible for much of the turmoil; not to mention the partying.

Everyone believed that I was going to get a long sentence, that I was destined to do some hard time.

At my court martial proceedings, I met with a lawyer from the JAG unit, and he assured me that if I wanted to remain in the United States Navy that I could do so.

Taking his advice, I plead guilty to fighting, Unauthorized Absence, disobeying orders, possession of nunchaku's sticks, and another prosecution for possession of a .22 caliber pistol (for which I had already been sent to C.C.U., constituting a blatant case of double jeopardy).

The judge in my case told me that once my sentence was served [that] I would be sent to another ship in the fleet. I was handed down a sentence of thirty-nine days hard labor.

I felt that I had caught a decent break, especially when considering the mayhem that I had been involved in.

CHAPTER EIGHT

I resigned myself to serve my thirty-nine day punishment and rejoin the fleet. I was told that I would get a sea duty assignment, stationed aboard another Spruance-class destroyer in the Engine Department.

Having a fresh start aboard another ship was my goal. I had seen a lot and experienced some hard situations in my two years in the Navy. I was fast approaching twenty years of age. I wanted to get squared away.

My idea and hope was to pick up the pieces of what was left of my enlistment. Even if I did not re-enlist, at least I could be discharged under favorable circumstances.

I reasoned with myself that I wanted to put aside the wild "partying." Too many problems had come my way when I was drinking and stoned. The dire consequences outweighed the immediate euphoria of some crude substance.

Expansive and large were the dormitories in the Brig: A-Dorm, B-Dorm, C Dorm, and D-Dorm. There was close to one-hundred men in each dormitory. And then there was the "lock-up wing" for segregation and isolation (solitary confinement).

In the general population at the Brig I was reconciled with Earl Bennett and Keith Hurie. I met Derek Flack (who was in the U.S. Air Force and from Washington, D.C.).

Together, the four of us were partners and "cut buddies" in D-Dorm. ("cut buddies" meant that we slept in racks or bunks that were side by side, the space between being "the cut"). No one was allowed to come into our "cut" without asking permission from one of us.

I unpacked my single box of meager possession and settled into the routine. I resigned myself to do my short stint of 39 days and get out.

The rules were simple enough: you worked, you did as you were told, and you minded your own business. NO TALKING AFTER LIGHTS OUT at 2100 (9pm), and NO LAYING ON YOUR RACK (bed) DURING WORKING HOURS 0800 to 1600 (8am to 4pm).

One day, after I had been in the brig two weeks or so, a young guard came through the dormitory and told me, in what I decided was a bad tone of voice, "Get off that rack."

I did not comply. I was still sore about the bigotry that I had experienced; and now I pre-judged any southern accent or voice to indicate discrimination. But I was wrong.

That was the cancer of bigotry. The few bad times of my experience had eaten a raw spot into me and spread; developing paranoia, not to mention a bad attitude and negative responses. Just like any disease I was infected.

When I did not comply with the order, the young guard walked away and went for his whistle that was attached to his shirt pocket. When a guard blew a whistle, it indicated a problem and all available guards would come running to deal with the problem. When they came they would come with hickory clubs in hand, and heads would get busted open in accordance with solving the problem.

He went for his whistle and I bolted from the rack. He saw that I was going to attack him and tried to run, fumbling for his whistle, and in his wrought panic he stumbled and fell, still tugging for his whistle that was now caught in his shirt. And then I was on him. He tried to shout an alarm, and I hit him with my fist.

My temper raged out of control. I saw his face and there were tears freely running from his eyes. Above the heat of my anger I could hear other guards coming. It was the "goon squad."

The goon squad was a special trained crew who primarily worked in the segregation and isolation unit. They were all big guys.

One of them rushed in at me, I threw a left hook and he buckled and went down. Spinning on my toes, I lashed out with my fists at another one of the goon squad, my fists landing squarely on his chin. He also went down.

They surrounded me. But they didn't move in on me right away, wary of the punches that I had thrown at their friends; none of them wanted to get hit. Realizing this, through my rage, made me feel strong. It was a crazy sense of bravado.

I tore off my t-shirt. Dared any one of them to try to touch me. I was a young man out of control. The Warden appeared and talked me into calming myself.

I was escorted out of D-Dorm and taken to the segregation and isolation wing of the Brig. The cell block was a forlorn section of the brig. Inside the segregation wing there was no activity and no signs of life. All the prisoners were locked inside their cells.

Entering the cell block willingly, I was suddenly jumped by a phalanx of guards. I was able to fight back. But it was a short fight. There was more than a half-dozen guards, all Petty Officers and Marine's. They pummeled me good.

Too many arms and fists to stand against. When I went down on my knees, I knew the battle was lost.

Completely down now, my torso and head took the scuffle and thump of their boots as they kicked my ass into submission. They kicked me real good.

I heard one of the marine's shouting, "You asked for it! You asked for it!"

Guards wearing gas masks appeared. Guards not wearing gas masks ran. Suddenly I heard a loud voice shouting, "Use the gas! Use the gas!"

The loud discharge of a canister of CS tear gas was fired into the Double O Cell where I was floundering from the beating.

I remember the canister of tear gas spewing thick gas and whirling crazily about the deck of the Double O Cell. I tried to grab it and kick it. My eyes burned and screamed with tears of fire. Defeated, I screamed and thrashed about. I remember my legs kicked twice.

Everything went dark.

CHAPTER NINE

When I regained consciousness, I was naked.

My head cleared and I remembering thinking, 'The marine was right, I had asked for it,' and they gave it to me.

I was trussed in a chain around my waist with handcuffs, leg irons were shackled around my ankles, and my twenty-year old body had been kicked and punched until bruised and dirty.

I don't remember the end of the beating, but it must have been a short beating, for if I had been beaten for a long time I may have required hospitalization. Still, dried blood was caked on both my lips, and the tissue around my eyes were puffed and swollen.

With no mirror nor reflection all I could do was feel the swollen flesh with my battered hands, and the flesh around my eyes felt big as cupcakes.

Written in the Uniform Code of Military Justice and enacted into administration as punishment the following decree: "Confinement on bread and water or diminished rations -- not more than three days and only on grades E-3 and below attached to or embarked in a vessel (U.S. Navy and U.S. Marine Corps only)."

For the fight that I had started in D-Dorm I was sentenced to fifteen days solitary confinement on bread and water. My clothes and all possessions had been taken from me.

I was naked. I would remain naked the entire time. "Strip Cell" is what it was called.

For three days, I would be given meals consisting of "bread and water," for one day I would receive regular meals, and then for more three days I would receive "bread and water" again – until the fifteen day period had lapsed.

Fifteen days bread and water.

The hole in the center of the floor stank of human waste. Reeking smells of piss and shit was maddening. The bread and water was pushed through a slot at the bottom of the solid steel door that caged me inside.

With my throat burned raw from the tear gas I couldn't eat for two or three days. I sipped from the two quarts of water that was given to me three times each day. After a couple of days, I began to lose track of time. The lights never went off. There were no windows in the double-O cell.

Other men were locked in the double-O cells. We never spoke from cell to cell. But I could hear screaming. I could hear someone singing songs.

Frequently, I could hear the Goon Squad, smell remnants of tear gas. Sounds of the Goon Squad were accompanied by the ruckus of someone being beaten. Sometimes I heard the Goon Squad up close to the cell, and noise of someone being dragged along the path of the cell block tier.

Losing track of time was strange. I did not know day from night. Time was nonexistent. And then I became constipated from meals of dry bread that I was being fed.

With constipation came pain. In a few short days I lapsed into unconsciousness. Not being cognizant, I suppose they found me balled in a fetal position atop the cold concrete that was the deck of the cell. Being curled into a fetal ball gave me an idea of warmth (in a place that was cold).

At the hospital, and only after the doctors there put up a stiff argument, was I taken off the bread and water diet. I was told that the doctor made it a direct order. I stayed in the hospital for two days before being taken back to the brig.

Back in the brig I was taken straight back to the double-O cell that I had been in. I thought I would be go back on the bread and water diet, but this was not the case. I was given regular meals. I had been sentenced to thirty-nine days hard labor in the brig.

The bread and water punishment had been imposed without due process. I have no explanation for this. Neither do I have any reason to complain. I had acted like a jerk. I had been errant and obnoxious – and I paid the price. A good price.

After the bread and water experience, I caused no more trouble. The penalty was very effective.

Earl and I were released from the brig on the same day. Coincidence. A grand reason for a grand celebration. Both of us withdrew a lot of cash from the credit union, and we hit the town of Charleston at full speed.

One block outside the Gate 3 of the U.S. Naval Station there was an LSD connection that was being run out of an arcade.

We copped fifteen hits of baby blue micro dots (very small pills), we chewed and consumed two hits each, and we washed them down with Johnny Walker Red scotch. We felt that we were ready to take on the world.

In downtown Charleston, we rented a hotel room. Our plan was to call up these twin sisters that Earl was acquainted with, Penny and Betty, and together we would drink and party for a couple of days in the hotel room.

Earl was on the telephone when the LSD started to take effect. He told Penny and Betty that we were doing acid – and they adamantly refused to come down to the hotel. I couldn't believe it.

The twin sisters wanted no part of the LSD, neither did they want to be around us while we were high off the acid. They were afraid. Frightened by the unpleasant stories they had heard about acid. They hung up the phone on Earl and refused to answer any more calls.

We laughed for a long time as the acid took full effect. On foot, we took to the streets, walking through Charleston all that night and into the next day. In my mind the acid made the sky seem alive with activity.

It looked like we were walking into the stars and planets and cosmos. Intoxication from LSD was a strange experience. It was not an experience that I particularly enjoyed. I took the acid because it was available.

Choosing to take the LSD was a foolhardy, hasty decision that I made in the aftermath of abject circumstances and events.

In the end the LSD was a bad experience. The drug did not provide the balm that I sought. My wounds lay open and festered beneath the raging delusions that beset my mind. Drugged out of my mind I cannot retell exactly what happened while intoxicated, nor compile any sequence of events for this period.

Bad scenes haunted me. Bad decisions made me feel worse. The brig, the beatings, the bread and water, the solitary confinement, the hospitalization from the constipation, and other bad scenes. All these negatives combined made me feel rotten inside. Rotten about life itself.

A week later the "celebration" of being released from the brig was still going on. Earl and I found all the acid that we could. If anyone had acid, we would buy all of it. We didn't sleep. We collapsed.

When we awakened we started right where we had left off. Empty liquor bottles were strewn about the hotel room. The LSD was masked with names that meant virtually nothing, "Orange Sunshine", "Goofy Blotter", and "Red Dragon Windowpane."

When the money ran low we retreated to the transit barracks at the Naval Station. We were both assigned to this barracks while awaiting activation of orders to report to different ships in the U.S. fleet.

My orders were for the USS Radford, another Spruance Class destroyer, that had its homeport in San Diego, California, and Earl was going to a supply vessel located in Subic Bay, Philippines.

In the barracks, Earl and I arranged to share a room. There were two other sailors assigned to this room as well. They were both white guys and we seemed to get along well. One of the sailors would party with us, drinking whiskey, smoking a joint of reefer, that kind of partying.

The other sailor was a Third Class Petty Officer, and NCO as it is known, and he was standoffish, kept to himself. But he wasn't rude or unpleasant. I suppose he was concerned about his career in the military service; which he had every right to consider. He seemed to be a guy who didn't want trouble.

Late one night, Earl and I burst into the room. We were zooming off LSD and whiskey, but the peak of the hallucinations had subsided. Still, we were wasted. Starting right in, we turned on all the lights, laughing and shouting and cursing.

My attitude was at a terrible low point. My behavior was irrational and out of control. I was obnoxious and bruising for trouble.

The Third Class Petty Officer protested and challenged us. We were making too much noise and disturbing everyone. In a drug fueled rage I went berserk. He tried to fight back. I beat him with a lot of punches to the head and face and drove him back to his bed, where he collapsed and stayed down.

I stood back. Talking big and tough, I dared him to report me, threatening him with more punches. In a hardened voice I told him that, "I been to C.C.U., I been to the brig!" I screamed, "I was on bread and water!" and I rambled on that consequences meant nothing to me.

It was tough talk. I was being a jerk. It was an expression that was not warranted. Yet it was talk holding on to the pain and discord of the sadness that I held inside.

Shameful emotion that overcame me. Suddenly, I felt like an antagonist. I was in the wrong this time. I was guilty of prejudging this white sailor. Was I no better than those who had bullied me? And prejudged me?

Realizing my guilt, I broke down and sobbed. In a loud voice, "I don't wanna go back there!" was my nerve rattling cry. I was distraught in a bad way.

Earl and the other two sailors', including the man that I had bullied, stood next my rack and told me to calm down and take it easy.

The sailor that I had been fighting checked my vital signs. He turned to Earl and mentioned taking me to the hospital.

He believed I was suffering from some mental illness; with good reason. He swore up and down that he would not report the fight. But he almost insisted I go to the hospital.

The next morning, I was called over to the Records Department. My transfer to the USS Radford in San Diego had been approved.

I was waiting for some paperwork to be signed when a young woman stepped into the office and told me, "They want you over at Mr. Hyatt's office." This was not a good sign.

Mr. Hyatt's office was on the first floor of the same building as Barracks 31. Mr. Hyatt was an older white guy. A civilian employee who kept records and charges on all misfits and sailors considered prone for trouble.

Mr. Hyatt started, "It's like this, Greg White. That Third Class that you punched at last night told everything. You're going to Leavenworth for at least 15 years for what you've done this time," he spoke without emotion; and he was referring to the United States Disciplinary Barracks.

I asked, "He told you what happened?"

Hyatt nodded is bald head, "He told everything. The drugs. The liquor. How you punched him. Everything. You're really lucky you're not in the Brig right now."

I was not surprised. The guy had every right to tell what had happened. I had been in the wrong. I had been a real jerk. "What about my orders to San Diego?"

"Sorry, White, had to put them on hold. The commanding officer wants to have you formally charged, but I told him that I had worked with you before, and I asked him to let me handle this.

They have found out that you do not have a school high diploma, they know you only went to the 9th grade in school and didn't finish that. Actually, you only completed the 8th grade."

Mr. Hyatt spoke with emotion, the words stung, and they became large words, "YOU DO NOT HAVE A HIGH SCHOOL DIPLOMA," and the words were big enough to fill my head with a sense of trepidation if not fear.

What could I argue? I had squandered my free time "partying" and chasing the loud scenes of the nightlife. My head was full of confusion. I was not able to sort through the haze that I had created.

Rather than buckling down and maintaining my military bearing, I had demonstrated behavior of a combative young punk. The lessons were raw. I had really screwed up this time.

Mr. Hyatt added, "Now look, Greg, they gave you a break at the summary court martial, gave you thirty-nine days in the brig. A big break. But you've thrown that away, man. This little fight puts you right back to where you started. The best thing for you to do is to take an administrative discharge."

An administrative discharge was known as "signing out" from active military duty. It was a method, likely overused at the time, to save the government time and money and the headache of having to deal with sailors or marines who had committed petty offenses.

"What?" I asked, "Sign out?"

"Yes. Sign out with this administrative discharge and you won't have to go to any court martial proceedings. This way you will retain most of your veteran benefits.

Technically, and it will be documented, you'll sign out because you don't have a high school diploma. I will note your credit for a 9th grade education on your discharge, although we found out you only completed the 8th grade."

Hyatt paused and added, "Not trying for the GED diploma hurts you, man. This is the best thing for you to do. It's an OTH discharge but in six months it will be upgraded to a General Discharge.

The commanding officer wants to charge you and have you at a court martial. Because you don't have a high school education on record they will let you sign out."

"But that's not what I want," I told him, I don't want to get out of the Navy. I want to stay in the Navy. Can I get a GED first? Can I at least take the GED test?"

"Too late. Now, Greg, I'm telling you, they're gonna take you to the brig, serve a new charge on you, give you a General Court Martial, and you're gonna get at least 15 years hard labor and a dishonorable discharge. You don't want that. Believe me, you don't want that."

The mere thought of going back to the brig was unsettling. The memory of solitary confinement in the double-O cells was maddening. It was a thought that produced bile. I had made mistakes that could not be undone. I cursed myself for being unable to cope with life. This was the end of the line.

I wanted to punch Mr. Hyatt in the face. But I didn't. I was a reckless young man – but I maintain my sanity. I knew that if I punched Mr. Hyatt I would face more bitter punished. Besides, I held nothing against him. None of this was personal.

I was tired. Tired of the battles that I had fought. Tired of getting spaced out of my mind with drugs and alcohol. Tired of the unknown pills that had fatuous names, names I couldn't pronounce.

Most of all I was sick and tired of having the shadow of minimal education dragging behind me like a burdensome bag of dirty rags.

I felt a disadvantage, a weakness in myself when it came to academics. Reading was an enjoyment, but I did not always comprehend what I read. I would try and try again. Putting the pieces of a sentence together in time. Having any kind of dictionary always helped.

"You do not have a high school diploma!" Words that rang loudly.

My service "did not amount to a hill of beans." But I was still a sailor. Many people saw me as being a bum. Some people pointed fingers and said that I was prone to making bad decisions. Quite a few threw up their hands in disgust at my behavior. With good reason. I had been a jerk. Overwhelmed with guilt. I caved in.

"Where do I sign," I said with defeat

Mr. Hyatt told me that I had to be off the U.S. Naval Station by 1600 (4:00 pm). After leaving Hyatt's office I went looking for Earl.

I went to the transit barracks. No Earl. I found my way down to the piers to locate his ship. He was nowhere to be found.

A little later I learned that his orders had come through and that he had joined his ship and was on his way to Subic Bay in the Philippines. He had left while I was dealing with Mr. Hyatt in his office.

I never saw Earl Bennett again.

Leaving the USS Moosbrugger DD-980 had been devastating. Hard to fathom leaving the 'Moose. And now, I was leaving the active duty ranks of United States Navy altogether. This was heartbreaking.

I had joined the Navy in search of a better way and a brighter tomorrow.

I had been a seventeen-year old kid with a five-dollar bill in my pocket – and a dream. A big dream of being a sailor.

My big dream had supported itself on a wisp of a prayer. But now it was all over. All gone.

I was a "screw up" (to put it mildly). I didn't have a dime in my pockets now as I was leaving for good. My pockets were empty. My clothes were wet and wrinkled. I felt sick.

Distinctly, I remember lowering my head and ducking my face to one side when I left the U.S. Naval Station, Charleston, South Carolina. I was soundly whipped and beaten.

Shame and degradation welled inside of me. Sometime during the worst of my melancholic mood, I had burst into tears and sobbed.

It was 9 October 1980. It was a day I cannot forget. I was twenty years old.

CHAPTER TEN

Sitting in a window seat on a Trailways bus, I watched the dark rain fall from the sky all night. From the pit of my own despair I struggled to breathe. With increasing speed, the Trailways bus winded its way out of the deep south.

A torrential rain fell from a dark sky. A sky dense with clouds that were full and heavy. I felt battered and overcome with failure. What a terrible way for a young person to assimilate the sum of his or her life.

Having had my butt kicked good, in more ways than one, I was going back to home Washington, D.C. An enormous sense of defeat hang like a cloud in the heavy rain storm of that very night.

The rain poured all that night. No way around it – I was whipped and beaten.

Returning home beneath the darkness of my own moods, no one asked what I was doing home again, if they did, I was heedless to give an answer. My world had transformed. I could not bring myself to tell anyone what had transpired.

No one knew that I had been discharged from the Navy. Nearly everyone believed I was still in the service.

I kept quiet and hunkered down in the dank basement at Grandma's house. Deeper into an unpleasant spirit of gloom I descended and flattened out.

As it had been when I joined the Navy I possessed very little; a couple of pairs of pants, a few shirts, a couple of jackets and a coat. And now I was right back to where I started.

Having no place to go, I went to my grandmother's house on Otis Street NE. Grandpa had passed away a decade earlier, but grandma kept the house.

My father was there. So was my uncle Junior. Frequently, my aunts and cousins would be there, coming and going, eating and staying over whenever we wished. Grandma's house was our family home.

This was the "safe place" where we sought refuge when the world outside overwhelmed us in some way – or when we just wanted to go and "Check on, grandma." Family members were always coming and going. Grandma was the best grandma ever.

I took refuge, likened as going into hiding, in grandma's basement. There was vast wealth of junk and clutter in grandma's basement. Heavy layers of dust made the stored junk seem ancient with age. I found an old folding cot with a lumpy mattress in grandma's basement.

In the basement I began having bad dreams about C.C.U. and the brig. I remembered being kept naked. I thought of the bread and water diet and forced myself to think of something else. Bad memories turned into bad dreams. A quart of cheap beer or a pint of cheap gin helped me sleep. The dreams of being beaten left me in night sweats.

Right away I began taking long city bus rides and drifting through other parts of the city. I'd go into public libraries and read newspapers and magazines and books. I was thinking of the magnificent ships and vessels that I had left behind in the sea port of Charleston.

I thought about how remarkable the small boats and the hand crafted "bum boats" in the harbor at Port Au Prince had looked. It was a time that I missed. I'd find books and read what I could about the life that was, seemingly, behind me now. I studied what I could on other sea ports.

During this time, I discovered the history of Jackson Wharf in New Orleans. Briefly, I stoked an idea that I could make my way to New Orleans and sign on a ship as a crew member, after all I had some shipboard experience. The idea of going to sea continued to be an important aspiration. I was curious about whether I would be accepted.

I could catch a Trailways Bus. I could hitch a ride. Not wanting to travel all the way to Louisiana and fail, I procrastinated.

Indecision on whether to travel to any seaport overwhelmed me, but I was still reading and rereading about the sea ports, some ports I had visited, and some ports that I might visit. My ideas of running away again were full of color.

Up on the avenue I would hang out with my friends for a while. Rhode Island Avenue and Thayer Street NE was where we frequently met. Drinking and smoking reefer. We all had ideas and dreams.

Rhode Island Avenue NE, from 14th Street NE to Eastern Avenue NE was pretty much our everyday area. By no means would we considered a street gang. We were a neighborhood group of young people who stayed close to the streets, spending our time and money chasing the life and the party scene.

Sometimes we worked for our money, sometimes we hustled: Theresa and Stephanie, Butchie Lee and Doris, Junior and Phil, Chink and Tony "Chicago" Love, and of course there were a few others that were part of this group of friends.

While I had been away in the military Theresa and Stephanie and Bing had discovered heroin.

Talk of going uptown to the area of 14th & U Streets NW to "cop some dope" was nearly the number one topic of their conversations.

In the beginning they were snorting the strong white powder. Before long they were skin popping and then mainlining the illicit drug into their blood stream. Shooting dope was becoming popular to my generation of friends.

The small street bags of dope had names. Trade-like names to indicate a specific person or group of people who sold the drugs. Some of the names that were popularly used at the time were: BLACK TAPE, 747, THRILLER, HANG 'EM HIGH, BROWN TAPE, SHAGGY DOG, DIRECT HIT, BLACK BUSTER, MURDER ONE, BILLIE JEAN, and RED TAPE.

No doubt, other names were invented. It was colorful but ominous. These small bags of dope were deadly, and the lifestyle that promoted street heroin was dangerous.

Many young people were shooting dope or shooting "bam" or injecting a combination of both narcotics. "bam" was a big deal on the streets of Washington, D.C.

Bam was preludin (stamped with BI62) pills, pink in color, and was used as a weight loss medication. It was a cheap derivative of the amphetamine family.

Mainlining bam would give an energetic rush to the senses, a feeling of energy, and loss of appetite and the loss of sleep. A person who used a lot of bam could go for days on end without sleeping. "Crashing" came in the aftermath.

There was dope and bam everywhere. But I had enough common sense to stay away from heroin, and not wanting to become a dope fiend I began to slowly distance myself from the Rhode Island Avenue crew. I would still hang out, but I would not use heroin. I would limit my time spent hanging out. It was a well thought out choice I made.

Heroin addiction was unpleasant, not to mention frightening. And then again, my friends would not share their dope with me - whether it was out of concern or out of personal hunger for the narcotics. Probably a combination of both reasons.

In time, on my own accord, I began to experiment more than ever with pills when they were available, or when they were offered to me.

In my naivete I reasoned that pills were safe to use. My knowledge of pills was something I picked up during my Navy days. Uppers. Downers. And probably some "homemade" pills that had no distinction.

I tried to hide this behavior. Drug abuse was nauseating. No one wanted to be identified with the shame of using narcotics. However, getting high wiped away the shame.

During late fall and into the winter months of December, January, and February, I took on small jobs; working for "day labor" companies that paid five dollars an hour.

When not working for these labor outfits I would spend time in libraries and find works associated or related to seafaring. Just like when I was a teenager.

I was no longer a sailor, but I could dream, and I had my memories. The life I had known in the Navy had been gratifying. The discipline, with punishments included, had changed me. A great sense of survival developed and grew inside me.

When I recalled the "bread and water" scenes, I shivered. Yet, desperate for relief, I was mindful that I had created that horror of my own volition. Taking a drink or swallowing some pills helped me to forget, helped me to sleep soundly – until the stupor faded. And then I was right back to where I started.

From time to time I panhandled; begging money from strangers on downtown streets.

When the weather began to warm I drifted towards the street more and more. Being on the street was not that bad; anyplace was better than being in C.C.U. Or in the Brig on "bread & water."

Keeping my few possessions at grandmother's house, I took step after step into the streets, into the world of homeless people; befriending another group of young people in the downtown areas of the city.

Living on the street was as free as many of us would hope to be. People were friends here. Likely it was the common thread of needing food and shelter that solidified these bonds.

These new friends, for the most part, were a homeless lot. Those who weren't homeless had, seemingly, chosen to be social outcasts.

Rag-tag revolutionaries and hippies left over from the 60s and the 70s still populated the Dupont Circle NW area.

The punk rocker scene was alive, and the punks openly congregated and fraternized with the has-been revolutionaries. Within this crowd were ex-pimps, former prostitutes, and alcoholic suburban dropouts. A scene left over from the former decades. A real melting pot of black, white, Hispanic, and Asian people. Nobody seemed to care about skin color. We were just living.

One thing is certain: no one expressed concern about where the day or night seemed to take them. In this circle, being homeless was okay, if not "cool" to be on the street. In those days one could be homeless and blend in with the crowd; no one suspecting that [you] were indeed homeless.

But no matter the rhyme nor poem, I began living on the streets as a homeless person. Sitting in the parks and squares of the city allowed me to re-charge my young spirit.

This is not to say that there were no rough moments. In low spirits I would wander the streets of Northwest in the District of Columbia, sometimes for days on end, considering all the world moving around me.

Consideration for my own place in the world as nearly always a forethought.

My days were long and lonesome. Flop houses were still around for $3 bucks to $10 bucks a night. A rickety cot in a flop house meant a warm shower and a warm blanket. Maybe an old pillow. For a couple of dollars this was a good deal.

If I needed a shower in a desperate way, and when the weather was warm, I would get a piece of soap, and late at night I would go into the backyards of houses and use a garden hose to rinse, soap, wash, and rinse again. Being clean was important.

Drinking cheap beer and liquor only served to make my breath stink. No help there. Having a lucid mind allowed me to tolerate my own sanity in a manner that suited my dispirited state.

For some time, I gave up drinking alcohol and smoking reefer. I wasn't having any fun. What was the use of getting stoned when there was no party? No enjoyment? Besides that, I could use my money for food, a flop, or matinee movie.

Befriending other homeless people or people on the street, I learned of several places where a good meal could be had for free of charge: Zacharias Kitchen, S.O.M.E. House, Miriam's Kitchen, Bread & Fishes, Saint Stephen's Church, and the well-known McKenna's Wagon (named after the late Reverend Horace B. McKenna).

Each day at 5:30pm the McKenna's Wagon van would arrive at 18th & M Street NW, where there is a small city park with a statue of LONGFELLOW, and the McKenna's Wagon would feed anyone who was waiting in line to be fed.

Sandwiches. Pastries. Hot Soup. Blankets. Sleeping Bags. Soft Drinks. Hot Tea. All these staples were distributed free of charge to anyone who showed up.

Should they run out of food or other staples, which was a rarity, there was another McKenna's Wagon van arriving at Lafayette Square NW at 6 pm, and yet another McKenna's Wagon van coming to 11th & M Streets NW at 7:30pm.

McKenna's Wagon was a significant symbol of profound greatness in the District of Columbia that I knew during these days of strife when I lived on the street..

One day, while hanging around Lafayette Park, I met a guy who asked me where he could find a soup kitchen or one of the McKenna's Wagon vans.

He was a white guy who looked like he was lost. His clothes, like my own, were wrinkled and stained, and he seemed anxious and hungry.

It was in that moment that I saw we were wearing the same uniform. My sharp dress whites were gone. Now I wore the wrinkled and stained outfit of a tramp.

No doubt, the stranger and I recognized each other as being one of the same ranks. A couple of bums.

I said, "Just hang out for about an hour and the 'McKenna's Wagon' food truck will show up at 6:00pm."

I went on to tell him that I ate in the soup line all the time, and that I was waiting for "the food truck" as it was known on the streets.

The stranger was incredulous, and he beamed with expectation. We chatted for a few minutes. I learned that he was from Romania, and that he was subsisting on low funds.

When the van with the food came we got in line together and loaded up with sandwiches and scored a couple of blankets.

Satisfied now, the Romanian told me he was living on the street and asked me where a safe area in the city was to sleep on a park bench.

"This is it, man," I told him. "This is the safest area in D.C., the White House is right there," and I pointed across Pennsylvania Avenue NW in the direction of the presidential mansion. "C'mon, I'll show you around."

By the time we reach the 2500 block of Virginia Avenue NW, near the U.S. State Department, we had both revealed to each other that we were sailors! (or had been sailors)

This guy was a Romanian merchant seaman, and he had "jumped ship" in Seattle, Washington, made his way to the Nation's Capital by hitch hiking and riding Trailways' buses all the way. Eating raw hot dogs and cheese spread all the way.

His goal was to reach the Romanian Embassy in Washington, D.C., find some help or refuge, maybe settle in the U.S. Or, at last resort, broker a successful return to his homeland.

This was a heavy set of circumstances. It was 1980. Romania was still somewhere behind the notorious "iron curtain." I had befriended a guy who had defected for political reasons from a country with an unfriendly government. I looked over my shoulder as he told me his story.

Politics aside, it was his stories of being a merchant seaman that captured my attention.

He told me he was licensed deck officer, a Second Mate, and he had sailed in various deck related billets aboard several deep seagoing cargo ships. Sailing out of ports on the Black Sea, from Constanta and Odessa through the Bosporus Strait, into the Marmara Sea, on into the Aegean Sea, and finally reaching the broader reach into the Mediterranean Sea.

From what he told me I was enthralled. Here was another way of going to sea. I told him that I had been a sailor, an engine department sailor, and we chatted into the night.

Joining a "merchant service" as he called it sounded like a great idea. I asked him why he left? What of his family? And would they have him put into prison should he return to Romania? Would he be punished? Tortured? Or worse?

As I thought of these questions, queries that I was putting before a person from a country where human rights abuse was reported to commonplace.

I could not help but remember that I had been punished, beaten and, to some degree, tortured for breach of guidelines and codes that governed my own "service" to my own country.

Yes, I had broken the codes. I accepted my punishments and sucked it up. But how much pain did I have to give?

My thoughts would not stray. The barren confines of C.C.U., the bread and water meals inside the double-O cell was more than a mere recollection. I had been left beaten and naked on the floor of barren cells.

The collective punishments left a scar inside of me. A scar not yet healed. And I could never forget [that] I had a responsibility in each punishment suffered. With that I felt like crap inside.

With blankets spread neat, we fell asleep on long wooden park benches on Virginia Avenue NW. The U.S. State Department, and the security related to the government institution, loomed in the back drop.

The traffic along the avenue went by at a pace that seemed to parallel my young life, and with the sun rise came a sudden rush of everything from everywhere.

With the dawn of a new day I offered to show the Romanian sailor some other good places to eat; and places clothing could be found, and other safe areas where a park bench would make for a good sleep.

Daylight came, and off we tramped to the nearby "Miriam's Kitchen" (then located at 19th & H Streets NW) and joined many others for a hot breakfast.

For lunch it was "Zacharia's Kitchen" in the 1400 Block of Church Street NW.

For the evening meal we lined up again at 18th & M Streets NW for the 5:30pm "McKenna's Wagon" and the food that was distributed and shared.

If we were still hungry, or wanted a clean blanket, at 7:30pm we could tramp down to 19th & Pennsylvania Avenue NW and a "Salvation Army" truck with hot soup, sandwiches, blankets, and sometimes sleeping bags would show up and distribute what they had.

For a run of three weeks we shared a bond of friendship. I learned all that I could about finding my way down to some dock, signing onto a tramp freighter, and going to sea.

The idea of on the deep blue sea again burned inside my head. In libraries I found reference material on merchant ships and seafaring; but no real information on the process of joining a ship's crew. I had no reason to stay on the streets of D.C. Being a bum was beginning to get the best of me. Getting out of D.C. began to burned my senses.

It was during this time that I discovered, what I thought, was fascinating material on the French Foreign Legion.

For the first time the idea of joining the French Foreign Legion crossed my mind. I ran this idea pass the Romanian. He frowned and laughed. He exclaimed with a chuckle, "My life is bad enough as it is. I want no trouble. I want no trouble," and we laughed about it.

The Romanian sailor and I would have our breakfast at Miriam's Kitchen, all the while talking about our experience as sailors.

After breakfast we'd go our separate ways, and we'd meet again at "the truck" in the evening. The Romanian was spending a lot of time at his embassy, and at some U.S. government office.

Exactly where the U.S. Government office was he never shared, I suspected it was an immigration office or an FBI office. Wherever it was, he was making a concerted effort to finding a way to remain in the United States.

One evening the Romanian did not show up at "the truck." I could only imagine what had become of him. Had he been granted asylum? Or had he been deported to a fate within a dungeon? I tried to push aside thoughts regarding the later. I wished the best outcome for my friend.

I never saw the Romanian sailor again.

CHAPTER ELEVEN

She was brown and beautiful. Her face fresh and radiant. I had seen her around in the downtown area before. Her face I remembered from the park inside Dupont Circle, which was a common hang out area for many. Her name was Deidre.

As she sat on a park bench, and I on another bench, I couldn't help but look at her and admire the beauty that was appealing, yielding vigor, and yet delicate. She was looking my way. She smiled. This was my cue, me tell point to make my move.

"How are you doing?" I asked, curious about the response that I'd receive.

She smiled, "I'm fine, thanks."

"What are you doing out here?"

"Waiting for the truck," she said and smiled.

"Oh, yeah. Me too," I answered and relaxed some.

We began to chat and make small talk. It was getting close to 5:30pm. Other people from all corners of the area began to congregate and wait for McKenna's Wagon.

Deidre was from Northeast section of the city, and she told me she was "just hanging out", and that she had no real plans for the evening. Likewise, I told her that I had no real plans either, and I offered to get us a bottle of gin from the liquor store in the 1900 block of M Streets NW.

After we went to the liquor store, the sky grew dark, the wind blew with a chill, and I told her, "Look, I've got a place not far from here, a squat house, you wanna come?"

"Sure, why not," I remember her words with clarity.

The strength of the wind as it whipped at our faces and set a chill all around us. I reached out and took her by the hand and off we went, walking west on M Street NW, veering to the left at New Hampshire Avenue NW, and making our way to Washington Circle NW. This is how I met Deidre.

I remember feeling good holding her hand and a pint bottle of gin in the other hand. It was a quiet affair. We didn't talk much. The season was right. The gin and the wind made us feel good.

Deidre and I became close friends while we were living on the street. It was the "struggle love" that has been celebrated in song and dance. It is a special memory.

"Squat houses" were commonplace in this area of the city. There were a number of vacant rowhouses lining the streets in Northwest D.C. that were in nice neighborhoods.

The squat house I claimed for shelter was on Washington Circle NW, near New Hampshire Avenue NW. This was the Foggy Bottom and the George Washington University area.

It was a rowhouse, on a short block, and there was a maze of connecting alleyways behind and adjacent to the rowhouse. The rowhouse was sectioned into five apartments, including the basement level, which was a one bedroom apartment or flat that I had claimed.

When it was cold outside this is where I was sleeping. This is where I was sleeping when it was cold outside.

A fireplace was in the living room area. When the weather turned cold we stoked and burned logs. Wall to wall carpet covered the floors. The carpet was blue.

Using spray disinfectant, I cleaned everything for germs or bugs. I worried about rats but took my chances. The bed was full size box spring and two mattresses; this I kept stacked high with several blankets for warmth.

Running cold water was in my basement flat. The toilet and sink worked fine. With no light in the bathroom, I burned a large candle with caution. I didn't use the bedroom, which was in the rear of the flat and had only a small barred window that faced the alley. I didn't like windows that had no view.

A rear door let out to the alley, and there was a short set of steps to the front door that opened onto Washington Circle NW. The rear door was kept barricaded and booby-trapped with makeshift alarms. If someone tried to bypass a barricade and enter the "squat" my "alarms" would sound, and I would rush to run off the intruder.

The West End Branch of the D.C. Public Library was on L Street NW, and the WEST END 1-2-3 Movie Theater was nearby on M Street NW. Georgetown was west out along Pennsylvania Avenue NW (that merged into M Street NW).

When Deidre joined me at the "squat" her friendship provided me a sense of warmth and comfort. What a good friendship it was. We didn't have anything of material value, but we had each other. We smiled a lot and held each other close.

We would go down close to the Potomac River and watch the boats. Overhead there were jet airplanes in the sky.

We talked very little. Sometimes we would hold hands. But we held each other close and warm, sometimes we kissed, but it didn't seem certain that we were in love. When she laughed it was sincere and sounded special and good.

One day Deidre asked me for some money so that she could buy cigarettes. I gave her some money. She said, "Thank you," and walked away. She seemed worried about something. I turned and walked the other way. I remember looking back and seeing Deidre waiting for a streetlight to change before crossing the street.

Briefly I thought of going to her, but I turned and kept going my own way. I reasoned I would see her later.

But I did not see her later. Neither did she show up at the food truck or at Miriam's Kitchen for breakfast. My guess was that she either went home to her family, or she may have entered one of the shelter programs for women in the city.

For more than a few weeks I kept an eye out for Deidre. But she was not to be found. Neither did she did not come back to the squat house.

Another cold winter was on the horizon.

With Deidre and the Romanian now gone I no longer had anyone to accompany me to the soup kitchens. No friends to chat with. I tramped the streets alone now. Life had taken me through a lot. Mentally and physically.

The squat house no longer appealed to me. Being alone in a barren place was unsettling. Soon, I stopped going to the squat house. Besides, the scent of saved sandwiches had attracted an array of vermin. Large cockroaches scurried about, and in the dark it was being overrun with rats.

Day and night found me wayward and with no place to go. I wandered the streets again. I had truly become a reckless young man. I found places were clothing was given to poor people or homeless people.

When I changed clothes, I would wash myself in a public restroom sink, put on the clothing I had gathered, and trash the clothing that I had removed. No reason for me to keep dirty laundry. I had no place to wash or store the clothing, and so I discarded garments when they were dirty.

A couple of times, when the weather was warm, and beneath the shadows in the wee hours of early morning, I had taken a piece of soap and went into the back yard of an occupied house.

Using the homeowners garden hose, I would water myself down and lather myself with soap. I would wash and rinse myself. Changing my clothing I would leave and disappear into the cover of the shadows. Again, I would leave the dirty clothing behind.

For money, I panhandled, or, if I was capable of rousing myself early enough, I would go to places where "day labor" work was readily available; these one day job assignments paid $5.75 an hour, and a paycheck would be dispensed at the end of the work day.

This was just enough to put some money into my pocket. I would buy cheap liquor, a few illicit pills, and ride the city bus or subway trains.

Movie theaters were always a shelter that provided heat and the cover of darkness that was great for a nap.

I slept on city park benches. I found apartment houses a great place to locate a storage room or stairwell, and I would sleep in these places. Laundry rooms were warm, but there was too much chance of being discovered by someone washing clothes.

Wherever I slept, usually I would only spend one night, preferring to move from place to place. As anyone can imagine, sleeping on the street, or specifically on a park bench, was not always with a great deal of security.

Being safe was a big deal. Living a life where survival was paramount was beneficial when I found myself on the skids with no true home. Sleeping on the street was not for everyone. Physically it was tiring. Mentally it was exhausting.

I remember times when I would walk and tread the streets until I was bone tired before stopping to rest. This was my way of assuring sleep as opposed to lying awake and worrying myself into sickness. Living on the street was tough set of circumstances.

Bakeries and restaurants were a great resource for free food. I would linger in alleyways near a bakery and wait for bread or pastries to be discarded into a dumpster – and I would salvage what I could.

At one such bakery, a young kid about 12 years old, who was the son or grandson of the bakery owner saw me getting a loaf of French bread from the dumpster in the alley at their bakery.

We stood and stared at each other for a moment. I was embarrassed. The kid told me to wait, and he went inside and returned with a fresh loaf of French bread.

The loaf was still hot. I offered him a few coins, but he waved me away with a smile. For the rest of the summer, about once a week, I would return to the alley behind this bakery and the kid would appear and give me a fresh loaf of bread. I always offered coins. The kid always waved me away with a smile.

One night during a rainstorm I had found shelter inside the storage room area of an apartment building. I was wet and dirty. I wanted to sleep that night. But I must have made a noise loud enough for someone who lived in the building to hear me. The police came.

Roused from my sleep, I was shoved and searched, arrested and handcuffed. Taken to a police station I was formally charged with the offense "Rogue and Vagabond" and put in jail.

The police laughed and told me that this charge was a misdemeanor and I could go to jail for three years maximum if convicted in court. I was scared.

In court, two days later, the judge looked at the police report and charges against me, and said, "What is this? 'Rogue and Vagabond!' Nobody gets arrested for Rogue and Vagabond anymore!"

The judge shuffled through more papers, and then asked, "Who is the arresting officer?" But the officer was not there in court. The judge asked, "Where do you live?"

I told him grandma's address.

The judge said, "Then you are not a vagabond. The officer is not in court," he paused and looked around, "case dismissed!"

Life on the street was getting tough. Needing a bath, looking for food, trying to find a safe place to sleep at night, it was all a day by day struggle.

How I missed being a sailor. My Romanian friend had given me an idea. I found articles and books about seafaring to make myself feel better. Some of these titles were the same that I had read and re-read as a fledgling youth.

For a few odd dollar's I would catch a bus to Baltimore to spend the day looking at ships in the inner-harbor area.

Just the sight of a ship set my mind full of ideas of going to sea again. On docks and pier's, I had asked questions, but nothing came of my inquiries.

I had been told to try joining a sailor's union, and was even directed toward such, but after walking many city blocks and growing tired I abandoned the idea. Save it for another day.

The trip from D.C. to Baltimore was a short one. Promised myself that I would return. I wanted to find my way back to the sea. I had to find my place on the "high barbaree."

Wandering the streets, wearing holes in my shoes again, I found myself headed for another confrontation with choices. Bolstering myself, I feigned bravery, and took another step along a side street. I had to make some choices.

Little did I know, I was gambling, and the stakes at the gaming table were being raised.

CHAPTER TWELVE

It was late autumn, middle of the first week in December 1981, dawn was breaking across the sky, and the air was cool and frosty.

Butchie Lee was driving an old gray colored Gremlin and automobile zipped and sped toward an engagement that held an ominous and disquieting promise. Butchie Lee urged the old car forward as if he were a professional race car driver bent on heading into what was to become the final lap.

I was riding shotgun.

I watched the city landscape flicker past as Butchie Lee maneuvered the old car from one lane of the broad avenue to the next.

Suddenly we took the lanes heading south along the infamous 14th Street NW strip. Peering out the car window and I watched the prostitutes and the hustlers as we sped past. Butchie Lee caught a long set of green lights and forced the old automobile into a mad dash for the 14th Street Bridge and the city limits.

Deep into the suburban sprawl of Fairfax County we raced. On and on we went. Life moved fast now. A blur and swirl. The cold morning chilled the inside of the old car.

21 years old. A pistol came out. Money was stuffed into a bag.

Then it was over.

Outside again. I walked. I ran.

Before I knew it Butchie Lee and I were in the car and jetting away from the location that was in Fairfax County, Virginia. Turning onto a two-lane road, racing on, miles were clocked behind us. Fast and away we went down the road. We were going to get away. We were going to be loaded with cash.

Just ahead was a busy intersection where an interstate highway would take us running home back to the District of Columbia. It was just a matter of getting fast to the highway.

Roadblock. Police everywhere. Weapons drawn and pointing.

"Get out of the car, nigger!" one of the police officers screamed in an angry voice.

A few quick moments. I was out of the car. Jacked up onto my toes. Pinned against the old gray Gremlin. The cold air was brisk and stiff.

A large magnum revolver was thrust against the back of my head. I could feel the hole in the barrel of the weapon as it was jammed hard against the base of my skull by a Fairfax County Police officer - who quickly put the weapon into the hands of a female police officer and told her sharply, "If he moves blow his head off! If he moves blow his head off!"

My world went blank.

Several hours later I awakened form a troubled sleep. I was locked soundly inside a cold and barren jail cell. It was a solitary confinement cell inside the Fairfax County Jail. Grim stains marked the inside of the jail cell. The world seemed to float around me. I was lost.

The moments began to come back to me a piece at a time. I began to recollect the perilous events that had transpired that December morning. The firm reality of my predicament was harsh. Knowing that I held all the responsibility was sobering. I was cold and shaken. I was scared, yet relieved that I had not been killed.

Special Agents from the Federal Bureau of Investigation showed up and joined the Fairfax County Police detectives. I was taken into a room and questioned. The Special Agent in Charge and one of the police officers raised an eyebrow when I told them that I had been discharged from the United States Navy just over one (1) year ago. I felt like a dumb kid. I was 21 years old. With no criminal record.

A police officer asked me, "Why did you get discharged from the Navy?"

I told the truth, "I got into some fights, and I didn't graduate from High School."

The police and FBI guys looked at each other. I knew they would check all of this out, but I had nothing to hide. It was too late for any deceptions.

The FBI Special Agent asked, "You were in the Navy until last year?"

"Yes," I answered.

The FBI Special Agent said, "Well, you did it now."

"What do you mean?" I asked, still out of touch.

"You robbed a bank. You in the big time now, brother. The 14th Street Bridge is twenty-five years away for you," he responded. "But let us talk about this and look into it all. If this is your only offense, we'll see. It's bad. But it's not the end of your life."

I didn't feel like I was "in the big time" at all. I just felt scared and stupid. After the interview I was led back to the jail.

Later, after discerning that I was not a professional bank robber, not a member of any criminal ring, the FBI did some paperwork, and decided to pass my case over to the Office of the Commonwealth Attorney for Fairfax County, Virginia for criminal prosecution. I faced a penalty of "No less than five (5) years and no more than Life in the State Penitentiary House of the Commonwealth of Virginia."

I was going to prison. Much of what I had heard from the streets about jail and prison was sensationalized or blown into a bigger picture than the reality. No doubt, I was keen about the people I would meet and encounter in prison. I reasoned that fights would happen.

From what was told word-of-mouth on the streets, there was a maxim I recalled, and that was: "There is no such thing as a fair fight in prison. To put up a losing fight was better than putting up no fight at all."

Robbing a bank was one of the crimes that carried a sense of boldness. I suppose this is what the FBI agent meant when he told me, "You in the big time now, brother." But I did not feel "bold."

The warped sense of "bravado" I had about robbing a bank was the worst set of ideas that I have created in my entire life. It had been a perilous, frightening experience for everyone involved.

Early one morning, while in solitary confinement in the jail, one of the jail guards came into the cell block and announced, "Does anyone want to take the G.E.D. test?"

A few prisoners said "no", some said "yes", and when it came my turn to answer, I stood at the cell door, and I said, "Yes."

I had not studied for the G.E.D. examination, had no preparation, but I had nothing to lose by taking the exam.

The exam would be given, over the course of two days, in one of the school classrooms that in the academic area of the jail. The jail library there. The thought that I may be able to claim a book to read crossed my mind. Having a book to read was very important in jail.

I told myself that I would pay close attention to the questions. With a deep breath, I sat down with the exam on the desk before me. Taking my time, I put aside tough questions, and returned to them later. I couldn't help but think of the battery of exams that I had taken upon entry into the U.S. Navy.

The two days of respite from the solitary-confinement went by fast. I was fortunate enough to pick up a couple of books from the jail library as I went to and from the classroom where the exam was being proctored. And then I was alone again. Back in "the hole."

Seven days later I found out my scores and result of the G.E.D. examination. I PASSED!

I now had a High School Diploma in my hands. It was cutting with irony that one of the factors closely related to me "signing out" from military service had been my lack of a High School Diploma or a G.E.D.

And now, in jail and awaiting criminal court proceedings, with a prison sentence hanging in the balance, I had earned the earned the high school education that I so desired. For me it was a milestone and a reason to feel good about something in my life.

I remembered how I had remained in the 8th grade, languished in the 8th grade. I recalled lowering my head in my classes, and the sadness of being 16 years old and still in the 8th grade.

But now I had a General Education Diploma in my hands. This was a great accomplishment for me. I felt I could step out of the shadows, if only for a few savory moments.

In February 1982, I stood before the Circuit Court of Fairfax County in the Commonwealth of Virginia. It was an affair that was mild and without sensationalism.

The handful of offenses, to which I entered a plea of guilty were singular violations:
1.) robbery (savings & loan company)
2.) weapons violation
3.) statutory burglary

I stood up and addressed the court, taking responsibility for my wrong doing. Briefly, I stated that I had been in the U.S. Navy and discharged for not having a high school education and for being rebellious.

I apologized for breaking the law. I told the judge that since being in jail for 2 months I had passed the G.E.D. examination. The judge wanted to see proof and my attorney took a copy of my G.E.D. certificate to the bench.

It may have worked in my favor. But the jail house fights probably worked against me. On paper, my behavior appeared reckless no matter where I went.

For my violations of the law I received a total of sixteen years in prison, with five years suspended, this would require me to serve a total of eleven years. I returned to the county jail resigned to my fate.

It was the middle of March 1982. I was twenty-one years old.

CHAPTER THIRTEEN

One day I went to sleep in solitary-confinement in the county jail, and the next day I awakened to find myself in solitary-confinement in a maximum-security prison.

What I remember from prison does not make for a nice story. All the stories are the same. Some of the stories are atrocious. Other stories are not so inhumane.

Beyond the mayhem and violence, sadly, what I recall most about prison was the effective breakdown of the human spirit and the consequential loss of the human soul. But the strength of the human spirit was always there.

When I transitioned from one penal entity and moved to another penal entity – it was all the same for me. The same strong odor of stale urine stung my sinuses.

The post nasal drip and after taste was bitter. I tried not to swallow. I breathed in short inhalations. I forced myself not to gag. In jail or prison, the same nasty smell of funky pee was in the air. This filthy smell is something I cannot forget.

Being stripped search was the policy. No exceptions. There were times when prisoners resisted or "bucked", as the saying went, when it came to being stripped search. If a prisoner "bucked" there would be a fight between the prisoner and the guards. The guards always won these fights. Leaving the prisoner beaten and injured.

After being stripped and sprayed, all of us were put into a solitary-confinement cell.

The door closing on a solitary prison cell always rang loud with a note of finality. It was always the end of the line. Being inside of a solitary-confinement prison cell was like being entombed alive. No exaggeration intended.

Without emotion, gruff words from a captain of the prison guards was pointed, "Keep your mouth shut, mind your own business, and you might get out of here alive."

We were all thin and green. I remember Wardell and Arnie; and I remember them because they were D.C. guys like myself. Wardell and I would become friends over the years. But after our initial induction into the prison system I was not to meet Arnie again. Never heard word of what became of him.

Thinking about being sent "down the road," as it was frequently referred to, did not unsettle me as much as it would some prisoners my own age. My constitution was resolute. My spirit had been toughened by a list of hard times.

My time spent in C.C.U., the brig, and the bread and water had tempered me, and with these experiences I had a resilience unlike many of my contemporaries. C.C.U. Had been a hellish experience. I only reasoned that prison could only be made worse by the length of time spent there.

Having books or magazines or newspapers to read was important when in solitary confinement. All items of reading material were taken from a prisoner during the punishment phase of solitary confinement. A single volume of religious material was sometimes allowed.

Prison life was forlorn. Meals were awful. Without fail the lunch time meal was the worst of the food; always a sandwich of greasy cold cuts and a bowl of water stretched soup.

Insects were found in the soup. Usually a house fly or a cockroach. This was common enough to no longer incite alarm or outrage. Few prisoners complained about the roaches in the food. The guards would eat the food sometimes; they did not complain either.

Occasionally there would be a strange looking bug. One learned to discard the insects and eat what could be eaten. Of course, there would be some cursing, even some laughter, about the the insects. The disgust would pass soon enough. This was the proven way to forgo hunger pangs over the course of a long day.

Sometimes a prisoner would "go off" about the food; waging some intensified protest that could include banging or kicking the solid steel door of the solitary cell. The racket was enough to jar anyone awake or keep anyone from dozing off. Prisoners protesting in solitary was an everyday occurrence.

Cases of mental illness were very much apparent in prison. Seemingly, and with decades of observation (from what I saw), the breakdown of spirit and the loss of a soul usually indicated the loss of the mind.

Men were succumbing to mental illness all the time. Displays of human madness was commonplace. And I would think this is not at all surprising to anyone – especially to anyone who has been incarcerated or worked in corrections.

Throwing human waste, feces and urine was common in solitary. It was almost as though prisoners possessed a definitive fascination with human waste, or blood, or anything that was vile and unpleasant.

For instance, a small vessel of feces and piss was collected, hidden in some way, and left to set for a few days. This horrid sludge of filth would ferment into a small but ghastly smelling cesspool. Powerful smelling filth was used as a weapon.

Next, the prisoner in possession of the slop would calculate who would be the victim, and when would be the right moment to throw it. The dirty business was called "baptizing" someone. Guards and medical staff were the most frequent victims.

A guard would open a food tray slot and quickly be doused in the face with the filthy sludge. A nurse would bring prescribed medication to a cell and get then same treatment.

A prisoner, in hand cuffs, being escorted to a shower or to an out of cell medical appointment or parole hearing, would get much of the same treatment. No one was 100% exempt from being a victim of this vindictive form of assault with human waste. And there were times when handling feces could rage out of control.

Baptizing anyone was cause for immediate response by the guards. Mustering, the "goon squad" would dole out some form of summary punishment to whoever threw the sludge. A good beating was the norm.

Anticipating a beating, the sludge thrower would put on as much clothing and bedding as possible. This was some makeshift padding to soften the beating. But in every instance the clothing and padding would be stripped off and beaten away.

A beating could last from ten minutes or over an hour. The goon squad used clubs and boots. Different voltage strengths of compact or handheld electricity was used; cattle prods, stun guns, electric shields, and tasers.

Commonly, a prisoner was beaten from one cell to another cell, from one tier to another tier, and this could mean being beaten all the way to another building at the prison.

Sometimes the prisoner was beaten to the point of injury [that] they would be beaten to the infirmary or hospital.

Routines were mundane. The guards would handcuff a prisoner (behind their back) every morning after breakfast, 8am or so, and remove the two inch mattress from the jail cell. At 4pm or so the mattress would be given back to the prisoner.

Removing the mattress every day was done as a weakened form of abuse and torture. What other purpose could this serve? Having a mattress inside a cell was not affecting the safe and secure operation of the facility. Not in any way. In each instance when a mattress was taken from a prisoner, it was done with malice and mischief.

Wide expressive grinning could be seen on the face of some guards. It was a sinister pleasure for some of these employees.

Resistance to having the mattress removed was trouble. A prisoner would be subject to further disciplinary action at an in-house "adjustment committee," and subjected to summary punishments ranging from a beating perpetrated by a group of angry guards to being tear gassed.

Being stripped naked and strapped to an iron bed in chains (restraints) was another punishment.
As in the brig, a mob of angry prison guards was known as "the goon squad."

When they goon squad came it would be a no-nonsense response, and prisoners would be subjected to a fierce beating. No exceptions. The goon squad would hype themselves into a frenzy-like state of rage.

Having taken my goon squad beatings while in C.C.U. and the brig – I was never beaten the goon squad at any civilian prison. The lumps and scars I received in the military institutions lasted me for decades. I knew a whole lot better by now. And I never threw feces or piss. Not at all.

I spent one year in a super maximum-security prison. Called "super-max" by everyone. It was a quiet prison. With all prisoners locked away in solitary a tense, tightly wound sense of silence was routine.

When noises did arise, it was contained, stifled to a rant or scream of a prisoner from behind a solid steel door. Or the noise could be the thundering rumble and thump of a goon squad beating a prisoner and then dragging the subdued prisoner away. This was a rat pack tactic.

At the super max prison there were five buildings with four tiers of cells to each building. The buildings were laid out in a circle around a courtyard, with each building having its own recreation yard or recreation cages, which everyone referred to as the "dog pound" (because it resembled a dog kennel).

I was in Building 5, which was next to Building 1. Death Row prisoners were housed in Building 1. From the small window of my prison cell I could look out and see the Death Row prisoners playing basketball. They always seemed to be a tight-lipped group of cons, they never seemed to talk much.

Long term solitary-confinement ruined the minds of prisoners. I well remember the sounds and noises that seeped through the small gaps in the solid steel doors. These sounds were unpleasant. It was the sound of madness that breached the routine of silence.

Threatening noises. Volatile words carrying stench of fear driven emotion. The solemn threat of, "I'll kill you!" permeated the air every single day. "I'll kill you! I'll kill you! I'll kill you!" Always the threat of "killing" someone rang from behind some solitary-confinement cell door.

Prisoners who exhibited signs of mental illness would often be subjected to the worst of the worst treatment. And a great deal of prisoners held in solitary-confinement were, more likely than not, suffering from some classification or stage of mental illness.

Strange ideas affected more than a few prisoners. Talk of the prisoner who practiced demonology was circulated in prison; and there was often more than one such prisoner at each facility.

Wild fantasies captured the imaginations of many. Off-track or bizarre behavior, in some regard, was looked upon with awe.

A prisoner who knew how to make a "Ouija Board," or who could perform a séance, was spoken about in gossip-like conversations around the prison yard – or even in the solitary-confinement cell blocks. Solitary-confinement afforded a man the isolation of mind as well as body.

One such man had drawn an intricate and detailed board of arcane dimensions onto the floor of his cell. His name was Tarrington, and he relished having others perceive that he was out of his mind. He was a tall, lanky blonde youth, appearing to be the "all-American kid," but he was not. Not at all. His mental state of mind was unpredictable.

For hours on end he could be heard chanting or crying in a foreign sounding language that only he understood. Every night he would wail out in horrible voice's. The pitch and wail of his voice's alternated from high to low.

Sonorous grunting was frequent. Pentagrams and stars, numbers and alphabet letters attached to geometric lines crisscrossed the entire cell in which Tarrington was held.

He made these drawings in any cell where he was assigned. And he only came from the cell to take a ten minute shower, and only during evenings when the moon was full. The guards left him alone. Prisoners left him alone, too.

Tarrington and I were on long term ad-seg, and we were allowed reading material. He had lots of comic books and text books, and he shared them with me. In return, I shared what books I had with him. It was camaraderie and solidarity.

Tarrington spoke to me one day. I was in a corner cell A-16 and Tarrington was in cell A-15. Hearing the whisper of my name one day, I realized he was beckoning me to "the telephone." I wondered what he wanted.

Spreading a blanket on the cell floor near the two inch gap, between the solid steel cell door and the concrete floor, was our "telephone" as we called it. It was a method on communication.

Right away I noticed that he spoke quietly. Nearly whispering to others. But to himself he yelled and screamed in fits and languages.

One night while on the telephone, and chatting back and forth, Tarrington offered me a drink of an alcohol beverage that he had concocted.

I was not so surprised. We had all made "hooch" or homemade "mash" wine. Making mash wine was not a big deal, and it was good enough to get a man drunk. I had gotten drunk lots of times in prison – in solitary and in general population. And I was pretty good at making wine.

But Tarrington had something different this time. He told me how he had squeezed two sticks of Old Spice deodorant into a pulpy liquid that he was drinking, and he said, "Two sticks will get you drunk," and he laughed quietly, adding, "If you drink three or four sticks, you won't be able to stand up straight."

I thought this over. I wanted a drink. But I was wary to try drinking the pulp from two sticks of Old Spice deodorant. In fact, I was cautious about drinking anything that came from Tarrington. He was unpredictable and not to be trusted. It would be nothing for him to give me a drink of something toxic. He had bragged about his extensive knowledge of poisons.

I passed, saying, "No thanks, man, I can't stomach it." Tarrington said, "But the good thing is your breath won't stink," and he went on, "and your shit won't stink either." I asked him, "How do you know that?"

Tarrington, answered, "Oh, I smell it all the time. Smells just like Old Spice."

I remember an incident in solitary-confinement when the prison guards, dressed to the fullest in riot gear, wielding electric shields, wearing knee high rubber boots, gathered in the cell block on the lower level tier., which was called "the flats" by everyone.

I was in a cell on the second tier and had a clear view of the scene that was about to unfold. (the cell block was shaped like a wide letter V)

A prisoner known as "Wild Man" was refusing to "cuff up" and be escorted from the cell where he was locked inside. He had done something inside the cell, and the guards were adamant that Wild Man be removed from the cell. They wanted him to go peacefully. Wild Man would not cooperate. He could be heard cursing in protest.

The order was given to "take him" from the cell.

The steel cell door was electronically opened, and, just before the "goon squad" of prison guards rushed in to seize Wild Man – a massive horde of flies swarmed from the cell and into the cell block.

Thousands of flies buzzed and swirled throughout the cell block. The terrible stench, sickening smell of feces and urine was overpowering. From my cell I saw two prison guards gag and vomit before they turned away and ran. Flies were all over the cell block now.

Guards rushed into the cell and pounced on Wild Man. He screamed as he was beaten and prodded with stun guns. The brief beating carried on with rumble sounds. He was subdued in less than one minute.

Naked, he was dragged feet first from the cell, his naked body was covered in a slick coating of his own waste. Wild Man cried and screamed. The stench was unbearable. He was so filthy that the guards stopped beating him.

One of the guards shouted, "Shit is all over my shoes!"

More guards gagged and dodged out for fresh air. The floor of the cell block had a long brown streak of waste from where Wild Man had been dragged away.

I grabbed a blanket and blocked the cracks in my own cell door to try to keep out the strong smell.

No one knew why Wild Man had spread his waste all over the cell that he was in. Waste covered the entire cell floor. Waste was heavily pasted on all the cell walls.

Wild Man had lost his mind. Likely, solitary-confinement, over the course of a year, had driven him to this madness.

In his madness he had become transfixed with his own waste.

I remember Wild Man crying and shrieking in a primal voice. It was an awful display of a human being pushed far over the edge. Sometimes when one went "over the edge" they did not make it back.

Later, as it was told by prison guards, Wild Man committed suicide by hanging himself. He had been found hanging by the neck from a rope made from a bed sheet. It was a brief story. Not a lot to discuss.
I don't know why, but I wondered, 'Does anyone care about Wild Man?'

In other instances', on numerous occasions, prisoners had taken the blades from safety razors, fashioned themselves something likened to a crude scalpel, and made brutal efforts to disfigure and maim themselves.

Screams were sharp through the cell block. In agony these men cried for help. They cried and cried and cried.

The screams were always chilling, always invoking a great sense of danger. Everyone, guards and prisoners alike wanted to know "What happened? What will happen next?"

After the screaming prisoner had been taken to a hospital, some of the guards would always tell a version of the story.

In one such instance when a solitary prisoner had maimed himself, distinctly, I remember a guard telling, "There was blood all over that cell, all over the sink and toilet, all over the floor and walls."

No one, guards or prisoners could understand any of it. The screams had been horrific. It had been a brutal act of self-mutilation. Solitary-confinement had become a chamber of blood and horror. What mania had driven this human being?

Some of the men in the cells around me had been in solitary confinement for ten years, twenty years, and even thirty years. "Detroit Black" has been in solitary since 1996. At this writing, this marks twenty-two years in solitary confinement fir this man.

I did numerous stretches in solitary. The amount of time adding up to over ten years total. A decade of my life locked alive inside a tomb.

Longest consecutive stretch I did was nineteen months. On average I did six months to twelve month stretches of time in "the hole."

Being in solitary did not have a profound affect me; at least not an affect that I could notice or put into words. But I was not conscious of that sort of thing. Being "affected" never crossed my mind. I was just doing time.

The pain of being in prison, solitary or not, was a pain that would not cease aching. It went on and on. The beat of the drum was nearly always the same.

For a great length of time, I did not believe that I would get out of prison. It was just that bad. I did not believe that I would live long enough to know freedom again.

I resigned myself to live out the balance of my life in the close confines of a prison cell. It was not something that I readily thought of every moment of each day, but the thought was there.

Death would come from disease or violence. I would contract an incurable ailment, or I would be stabbed to death, beaten to death, or worse, on the hard expanse of some prison boulevard. And no one would bat an eye. Why should they?

My behavior was combative. Fighting earned me additional time added to my sentence. I had not choice but to live with it. I asked myself, 'Am I truly without hope for a future?'

Parole dates came and went. Every parole hearing was met with denial. In writing, ach year I was formally told, that I was "not ready to conform to society" and "not likely to obey the law."
As an option for release, every bid for a work-release program was rejected. Holding a thin piece of paper with "denied" or "rejected" written on it was surreal. It was as though my life did not matter.

Prison and parole officials conceded [that] I would not make good as a law-abiding citizen should I be released from prison in any manner nor form. Officials were convinced that to release me on parole or to a work-release center would prove foolhardy. I was a poor risk. I would not be successful.

My future was regarded as dismal and without hope.

But it was nothing so new. All around me, for nearly the full of my life, many people had been telling me, "You cannot do this," or, "You cannot do that."

Always there seemed to be a mouth poised in wait to refute or assail any idea or aspiration that I would offer or share. In prison this position seemed intensified. Encouragement was not given. It was a setting where to be countered or opposed was as common as breathing or drinking water.

Many prisoners held onto to dreams of a better tomorrow. But prison was not the place for optimism. With little deviation, prisoners were reminded, over and over, that any prospect for building what was essentially a "new life" was a virtual impossibility. Rejection and denial was the basis of any conversation regarding how things would be [on the outside] for an ex-offender.

One of the most important lessons I learned was that "rehabilitation" is a personal responsibility.

CHAPTER FOURTEEN

But there were positive examples of men and women, former prisoners, ex-cons if you like, who had been to prison and made good lives for themselves upon their release on parole or work release. These men and women had become, whether they knew it or not, beacons of hope – for those of us who they had left behind on the inside.

I formed bonds of camaraderie and friendship with men who "turned their lives around" and found stability through hard work and commitment. Some of these men had experienced a spiritual awakening, adopted religious beliefs, and held fast to what they saw as "blessings" in their lives.

Religion in prison was a big deal. Christianity and Islam were the most popular religions going. Walking the straight and narrow disciplines of religion and the tenets that were relevant to the "choice" of religion became the defining moment for many of these men (and for women, too, I'm sure).

I met religious people while in prison; humble and studious in manner they were. Having a belief in God was important for nearly everyone.

Yet prisoners who adopted a religious stance, or commitment, did not always agree with each other. I remember fights and sometimes extreme violence over religion. It was odd, but a part of the culture (I suppose).

Many times these disagreements were minute matters, boasting of knowledge gone too far, and at times ego's out of control.

Prisoners often possessed an incessant need to "prove" themselves, and this could sometimes manifest as a fight; verbal or physical. And fighting was a big deal in prison.

I developed bonds of camaraderie and friendship with several men who "turned their lives around" and found stability through hard work and commitment. Some of these men had experienced a spiritual awakening, adopted religious beliefs, and held fast to what they saw as "blessings" in their lives.

But who had the true answers?

Dredging memories to surface, or forethought, became a way and means to comfort myself. Thoughts, some long buried, allowed me to retain my sanity. These memories provided a balance of stability. I wanted to understand just what forces had allowed me to develop as I had. Memories also allowed me an escape or diversion from prison.

Self-imposed questions: 'Why did I get angry so often? Why did I resort to fighting?'

I would think of my family. Often this would start with a reverie of my mother.

Recalling my mother, I would paint mental pictures of how she deported herself, her mannerisms and demeanor, how she developed decisions in her young life, and her longing for "something better" in the world that stood all around her.

We were so young. The picture of the rest of the world cast a shadow that made our world of walking tough and "thorough" appear small, contained, and limited within a small picture frame. I remember being a teenager and trying desperately to survive.

I had a vivid memory of the day and time concerning the first friend of mine who had been killed to illegal handgun violence.

It was a school day in April 1975, and Jimmy Teasley was the one who told me the news, "Randy Barnard" got shot and killed last night."

"What?" I asked, thinking I had heard him incorrectly.

"Randy Barnard got shot and killed last night in Kentland. He was with Bobby and they robbed the Chinese Restaurant in the Shopping Center across the street from the Bowling Alley."

"What?" I was incredulous, or maybe I was shocked by the words I had heard just heard from Jimmy.

Later we heard more news: Randy and Bobby allegedly robbed a Chinese Restaurant at gun point and took cash. Bobby had the gun and as they ran from the restaurant there was an unintentional collision at the front entrance to the restaurant. The pistol fired twice. Randy was shot in the chest.

Together, Randy and Bobby ran across the street. Randy collapsed. Bobby stayed with him. The police came. Bobby was arrested. Randy was rushed to a hospital.

Randy Barnard was dead. He was fifteen years old.

The news of the tragic and unfortunate death of our friend and school mate Randy filtered like a cool wind through the neighborhood. It was hard.

We were all fourteen years old, fifteen years old. I remember walking around with a feeling of emptiness deep inside of myself. This entire incident was a reality that many of us were unprepared for.

Being young we were living our lives in pursuit of a good things in life, the good times, and the excitement of what the future would bring.

This death, though unintentional and without malice (at the hand of our mutual friend Bobby), still arose from the cause and consequence of a violent crime coupled with the use of an illegal firearm.

My mother, as did all neighborhood parents, heard the news concerning Randy and Bobby. Randy was dead at age fifteen. Bobby was charged in his death and charged with armed robbery.

Rightfully so, my mother began to put pressure on me, checking my behavior best she could.
My mother had been shocked and appalled over the death of Randy. She remembered him well, seeing him about the neighborhood and such, and now he was dead.

As a child, my mother had never spanked me. But now, as an unruly teenager, my mother attempted to discipline me. Our relationship changed. Things were becoming heated for me. In hindsight, my mother was doing what she could to save me from the street life.

I possessed vague ideas about my community and the world that buffered my community. My mother seemed worried that I was in some eminent danger.

She would stress to me, in a demeanor of importance, "If the police stop you, do not run. Tell them you are underage and tell them your name. Tell them my name. Tell them where you live. Call me and I will come and get you."

I remember thinking, 'Why should I be worried about the police?' But I kept those thoughts to myself. With more thinking I began to realize that my mother was giving me a life skill for survival should I have an encounter with the police.

I was fifteen years old now. Though skinny, I had reached the height of a man. Standing at 5'10" I could easily be mistaken for an adult.

Being a teenager was a tough experience. Trial and error. The mistakes I made were many. Not unlike a lot of inner-city kids. It was a hard-bitten set of situations to review – and only God knows how I survived those dire moments.

I spent nearly all my time in the street. Going to school in Maryland suburbs Spending weekends and holidays (at my legal residence) in the District.

Running back and forth along Rhode Island Avenue NE finding my way to 14th Street NW, being a part of the crowd, while being a spectator on the sidelines in the bazaar of the life that was to be found in these inner city areas.

Day by day, night by night, it was during this period in my young life when I began to stray towards the street life and negative behavior. In the classroom I was not much in the way of being a good student. Homework was never completed.

With frequency I was truant from my classes. Late nights in the street does not prepare a student for a long day in the classroom. I stayed out late every single school night.

Mannerisms and an attitude of not caring was my way during this period in my young life. I smoked a lot of reefer and I drank a lot of Wild Irish Rise wine. I became a rebellious and difficult teenager.

After a fist fight, I would slump into a state of sadness, and struggle with morose feelings. For diversion there was wine and beer. Books and magazines.

Occasionally there was a joint of reefer and the faintly bizarre hallucinations that came from the effects of using marijuana. In the books I found solace and a reprieve. From the reefer I found confusion and a misunderstanding of myself.

Late one night, a school night, I was walking with a couple of friends along a street in Dodge Park. We had left our clubhouse and were on our way to a liquor store to steal a case of wine.

Our juvenile method for stealing wine or beer was something like this: One of us would hold the liquor store door wide open, and two of us would suddenly grab a case of Wild Irish Rose wine and bolt from the liquor store.

If the clerk or proprietor chased us and caught us we would ditch the case of wine into the street and run away; if the proprietor grabbed one of us and tried to hold us for the police we would fight him off and run before the police came.

This night I was carrying a .38 caliber revolver stuffed down behind the belt of my pants with a windbreaker jacket pulled over my waist (to further conceal the firearm). I had just begun walking down the street with my friends when suddenly I saw my mother's car parked right there at the curb. I was shocked. I was mortified.

My mother jumped out from behind the wheel of the car and ordered me to get inside the car. I protested. On the sidewalk my friends snickered. My mother started to come at me.

With my head reeling I relented and got into the back seat, sitting behind my mother who was driving the car. I was high from smoking reefer and drinking wine; and I figured I would go home with my mother. Let things cool, and then sneak back out once she was asleep.

In the car my mother berated me. Non-stop she shouted and cursed and scolded me. She said something about how Randy Barnard had lost his life, and how I was going to end up just like him. Her exact words were, "You're going to end up just like your friend Randy!"

The .38 caliber revolver was uncomfortable in my waist and digging into my crotch. I was trying to adjust the pistol in my pants when it slipped over my belt and fell out onto the floor of the car. My mother saw the gun and screamed, "You've got a gun!"

My mother stopped that car in the middle of the street, turned around in the driver's seat, seized me by the throat and demanded, "Give me that gun! Give me that gun!" I had no choice but to give her the weapon.

She punched me in the face twice with her fist and drove down the street.

She went on a tirade now. She harangued me with every dire consequence in the book. She then exhorted that I would be in reform school or dead before I was 18 years old. I had been caught and there was no way around this situation. I was in shock.

She said, "I'm taking you straight to the police station! They're gonna lock your ass up tonight!"

After the car pulled into the parking lot of the police station and came to a halt, I opened the car door and jumped from the backseat – my feet hit the asphalt hard, and I took off running. I was gone. I ran as fast as I could for a long time.

My relationship with my mother deteriorated to a very low point. In fact, the relationship I had with my mother was nearly non-existent.

As I grew older my mother would beat me. Punch me in the chest. Use choke holds. Slap me around in my face. As a last resort she began locking me out of the apartment at night.

Thus, began a custom of "putting me out" to live on the street; my mother's way of punishing me. It was a callous and ineffective form of punishment, not to mention hazardous and not very safe. Living on the street was not without peril.

But still, getting put out on the street became routine. It was my punishment. And I had to suck it up.

With my mother working to make ends meet, she didn't have any free time to chasten me - so out the front door was her way to punish (with a smack in the face to carry me along). No doubt the factors regarding her youth determined a great measure in how she fared herself as a parent.

I had no place to go. But that seemed okay. Roaming the streets was much better than being in a juvenile detention center.

Walking the avenues, finding alleys and obscure side streets, learning where they went beneath the cover of night. With a handful of coins, I'd ride the D.C. Transit city bus for hours, venturing into distant neighborhoods, my eyes alert and searching with hope that I'd find something. Just what it was that I hoped to find is an uncertainty.

During the day it was much of the same. It was about this time in my young life when I began to discover places like The Library of Congress, the museums of the Smithsonian Institution, and I would even venture out to Arlington National Cemetery.

Having little or no money these were places where I enter for free. These were also places where I could have time to think. I was thinking about life. Thinking about how my young life was taking shape. I was only fifteen years old. How would I fare in the world as the years progressed? As I grew older? As I entered adulthood? What would I do with my life?

Going to sea was a frequent dream. Being a sailor would allow me a door to the rest of the world.

And then I was sixteen, and seventeen, and then I was gone. Getting out of Washington, D.C. and the immediate area was, really, a dream come true.

I thought of these things as I languished in prison. Revisiting my past allowed me a perspective, if only in memory of what was, that chances go 'round, and that dreams can manifest into something more than a daydream.

CHAPTER FIFTEEN

Prison life is slow. Day to day activities are only spotted with the excitement of letters from home, visits from family and loved ones, sporting events and activities, and the grand excitement of being released on parole someday. Other than that, there are only the fights and the riots that stimulate the senses. Being "bad" was how one garnered respect. For a period of time I dressed in combat boots every day.

An older prisoner, his name was "Abdullah", and he once told me, "Take a piece of paper and write down all the so-called tough man things that you have done. Write down all the fights. Write down all the knockouts. Write down all the beatings that you have suffered. Mark down the riots. Jot down and note everything that would support your stance and mark as a tough guy."

I looked at Abdullah with an eye that said 'I'm a serious dude, man. Don't waste my time.'

Abdullah countered my eye with, "Relax. Don't lose your cool. Think about this. Take your piece of paper with your list of formidable deeds, fold it up and stick it your pocket, go down to the supermarket, when you get out of here, fill a shopping cart with food and vegetables and goodies. Get all the things you like to eat.

Go to the checkout counter. Tell the clerk that you have no money. But you have this list of formidable deeds that you have participated in. See if this dreadful list of deeds will pay for that shopping cart full of food. Take this list and try to pay your rent. See if this list detailing your 'badness' will satisfy your medical bills."

He concluded, "In the 'real world' a jailhouse reputation don't mean anything. Nothing!"

When Abdullah spoke like this, we, younger prisoners, listened. These few words from an old con on the big yard never stopped ringing a small bell inside my head. This piece of advice did not go unwarranted. I started thinking about leaving my "badness" behind me when or if I were to be released.

Abdullah was from New York City, uptown in Harlem, and through his family and friends he was able to access the white pages in a New York telephone directory.

This was the conduit for me to procure addresses and telephone numbers to reach my partner, Bruce Clark, in New York, or at the very least connect with one of his family members. It had been several years since I had left the 'Moose. But that didn't matter, we were partners – and I knew that if I contacted the right "Clark family" that Bruce would respond.

I sent several letters to a few "Clark" residences in the St Albans and Springfield Gardens areas of Queens, New York. I remembered Bruce had a sister named "Jeannette" just as I had a sister so named. And so, I addressed a letter to the address of Jeannette Clark for Bruce.

It was a score. Within a matter of weeks Bruce responded. About a month later Bruce showed up at the prison for a visit. And this was how we were re-united to sustain our bond of friendship.

CHAPTER SIXTEEN

But there were positive examples of men and women, former prisoners, ex-cons if you like, who had been to prison and made good lives for themselves upon their release on parole or work release. These men and women had become, whether they knew it or not, beacons of hope – for those of us who they had left behind on the inside.

Parole dates came and went. Every parole hearing was met with denial. Every bid for a work-release program was rejected. Each year I was formally told, in writing, that I was "not ready to conform to society and not likely to obey the law."

In short, the prison and parole officials all conceded that I would not make good as a law-abiding citizen should I be released from prison in any manner nor form. I would not be successful. The faith that was placed in my worth as a person was on the low end of the scale. No one wanted to give me a chance.

To release me on parole or to a work-release center would prove foolhardy, not to mention the possibility or potential for violent crimes to be committed (at my hand). Prison officials and parole boards had effectively closed the lid on my file, regarding my future as dismal and without hope.

All around me people were telling me, "You cannot do this," or, "You cannot do that." There always seemed to be a mouth poised in wait to refute or assail any idea or aspiration that I would offer or share.

In prison this position seemed intensified. Encouragement was not given. Being opposed was as common as breathing or drinking water. Discouragement was an everyday thing.

We were prisoners. Convicted felons. Jailbirds. Vermin. Scum. Yielding no value than a piece of waste would have. It was commonplace [that] we were no longer a part of the human family.

There was the pretense and guile of many who became enamored with the "jailhouse reputation", and the aura of "Don't Mess With Me!" or "I'll hurt you real bad!"

Hurting people real bad became a sickness inside prison. Countless prisoners entered the jails or correctional facilities with a five year term or a ten year sentence - only to have their sentence increased by "catching more time" or "running time up" as the sayings go.

Many prisoners have increased their sentence, some to the point where they will never be released. The death penalty has been handed down in some cases.

The years went by slowly. The boredom grew. The monotony of prison life mounted. Reading and studying was my way. Sports and keeping myself physically fit helped relieve stress. Every so often there would be a fight, or a demonstration, or what could be detailed as a riot. People would get hurt and injured (prison staff and prisoners alike).

Time marched on in a way that became hollow and full of displays of emotion. Of course, there was a sense of shame (within). Few prisoners would ever admit being proud of their crimes.

Only the hard-core individual could express a lack of remorse for the damage caused by their respective crimes. And, again, there was the mentally ill that padded the general prison population(s). Mental health issues among prisoners remained a constant problem. No way to circumvent this; it was a fact of life on the inside (of prison).

As prisoners, we were indoctrinated to believe that we could not rise above our lowly station. Convicts were brainwashed into believing much of what was said or demonstrated (about them). Solitary was always the end of the line.

We had even failed inside prison. Solitary was the effective concept of being in prison within a prison. We had failed in society. We had failed in prison. We were useless. And that was that.

Bottom of the barrel.

CHAPTER SEVENTEEN

In the summer of 1997, while doing yet another long stretch of time in solitary confinement, I came across a section of newspaper. It was a book review.

The caption was bold, "SAILORS ON THE WINDS OF CHANGE: BOOK FINDS BLACK SEAMEN HELPED CARRY THE CARGO OF FREEDOM" by Ken Ringle (published in The Washington Post's Style section on July 24, 1997). The newspaper piece captured my attention in a great way.

The title of the book was, "Black Jacks: The Story of African American Seaman in the Age of Sail," written by W. Jefferey Bolster, a history professor at the University of New Hampshire.

After reading the review about the book Black Jacks I thought about my own connection with the sea. I thought about how I had been a young sailor once. My memory of what I had found as a sailor was special. The recollection of the camaraderie and the bonds of friendship that had surfaced from these relationships.

Out beyond the far reach of the shore, while sailing on wind swept waters, I had known what freedom was; not unlike many of the African and African-American men and women noted in Black Jacks.

In solitary-confinement, inside the cramped heat of a prison cell, I paced the short distance of floor space, reading and re-reading this scrap of newspaper. The story burned my imagination.

I had an idea. I would chance a postage stamp and send a letter to inquire more about the subject of book, and what chance, if any, there was that I could become a sailor again – and find my way back to the deep blue sea. Any chance, no matter the odds, would give me "something" to pursue.

I began to dream if there was any chance, no matter the odds, that I could make something worthwhile out of this idea. I wondered if there was a way, even a

There was no use in asking anyone at the prison – invariably I would be told "no" there was no chance for me to become a sailor. I would be derided as "foolish" to even think about being a sailor again. Besides, I was not only in prison, I was in solitary.

All around me, nearly the full balance of my life, numerous people had been telling me, "You cannot do this," or, "You cannot do that."

There was often a mouth poised in wait to refute or assail any idea or aspiration that I would offer. In prison this seemed intensified, prison was definitively a world where being refuted was as common as breathing or drinking water.

But the dream would not leave me alone.

Reaching for an ink pen I decided to make a bid to breach the barrier of prison. Being at the bottom of the barrel only served to strengthen my resolve. I pondered whether to send a message to Ken Ringle or to W. Jeffrey Bolster.

I wanted to know more about the book Black Jacks and the possibility of finding a place for myself in the maritime industries. I had to do something. Just a letter would be better than nothing.

Inside of a dated "World Almanac and Book of Facts" I found the address to the University of New Hampshire and drafted a letter to W. Jeffrey Bolster. I mailed the letter and waited for a response.

One week later I received his response. Jeff Bolster wrote a letter to me dated August 13th, 1997. It reads in full:

"Dear Mr. White,

Thank you for your letter. I am delighted that you are intrigued by the subject of my book. Clearly, you are a man who likes to dream, who feels called by the sea, and who likes to write. A man, too, who knows more than most these days about restricted freedoms. You are a soul mate with the men I wrote about in Black Jacks.

The brave, unchanging sea will be there when you get out. It is waiting for you. Good luck to you. I hope you're out soon, and hope that you find the circumstances and the strength to walk a different path."

The letter was signed, "W. Jeffrey Bolster, Associate Professor."

I wrote another letter. Asking more questions, specific questions. A few days later, again, Professor Jeff Bolster responded in a positive and encouraging way. This was the beginning of my new-found quest and ambition to become a documented merchant seaman - and find a place for myself in the maritime industries. Jeff Bolster and I began to correspond frequently.

Jeff offered me encouragement to pursue employment as a professional mariner, telling me in plain language, "There are quite a few ex-cons who work on ships as seaman." He was adamant about this, telling me, "I know this for a fact," regarding ex-cons working in the maritime industries.

My contact with Jeff, and his book Black Jacks, became the catalyst for me to reach beyond the barriers of prison; barriers that were both physical and psychological. Through this connection I was able to be introduced to other professional seaman.

With these introductions, I was able to form practical plans, taking sure steps towards going to sea again. My dream moved closer to becoming a reality.

Soon after my contact with Jeff, I corresponded with Captain William "Biff" Bowker, Captain Michael J. Schneider, USN (Ret.) of Project Liberty Ship - John Brown in Baltimore, Maryland, and Captain Daniel Moreland of the Barque Picton-Castle homeport Lunenburg, Nova Scotia, Canada.

Each one of these professional mariners offered advice and encouragement to me. All of them were in collective agreement [that] becoming a merchant sailor would be an excellent way for me to change the course of my life – give myself a future – and redeem myself as a human being and a law-abiding citizen.

My correspondence with Captain Bowker was especially memorable. He was living at the retirement home, "Sailor's Snug Harbor," located in North Carolina on the sea coast. He answered every letter and question that I asked of him.

The captain had been a sailor nearly his entire life. His maritime career began when he pushed off in the 1920's in whaling ships off the New England coast.

During World War II he had worked as Chief Mate and Captain aboard Liberty Ships and other U.S. Merchant Marine ships.

He was a veteran and survivor of the nefarious German Navy U-Boat campaigns known as the "Wolf Packs" and who waged terror on the sea in what is remembered as "The U-Boat War."

Over time, the letters I received from this old war veteran sailor waned and were no longer legible. His handwriting faded. One day I received a letter from the Captain that he had dictated to a nurse or other caregiver. He explained that his health was taking a turn for the worse.

The physical barrier remained intact. I was still incarcerated, and I would have to bid my time and serve out the remainder of my sentence.

Yet with an idea and a plan that constituted hope and redemption, I dug deep into myself, willing myself to gather the strength and courage to face down the barriers – no matter what the extent of these barriers were. I comforted myself with a resolve to become a sailor again.

Naysayers were all over me. I was encouraged to find a job doing construction labor. I was told, by family members and others alike, "No way you can become a sailor again."

But I said, "I'm going."

CHAPTER EIGHTEEN

In October 2003 I was released from maximum-security prison. I served twenty-one years and eight months.

I was now forty-three years old. I had twenty-five dollars to my name and a set of clothes on my back.

My mother, Mary Elizabeth, came to the prison to pick me up and drive me back to Washington, D.C. Throughout the long years of my incarceration my mother and father maintained regular and frequent communication and contact with me, and showed me the strength of commitment and perseverance.

My parents, young as they were, never gave up hope and belief that my worth as a human being was invaluable. My mother pressed self-assurance into me and provided me with great inspiration with the example of her undertaking of hard work and responsibility.

On 20 December 2003, my mother passed away in her sleep, less than two months after my release from prison. She was fifty-seven years old.

She had lived out the last two decades of her life holding out hope and prayer for me.

She often remarked to others, "My health is bad. I'm not well. But I pray that I live long enough to see my son Gregory get out of prison."

And she did.

I suppose she had given every grain of her energy and sincerity into that prayer - for me. And now she was gone.

At forty-three years old, I had never held a position of employment in the working sector. Theoretically, I was beginning my adult life. 43 years old and coming of age.

Soon after my mother passed, I remember thinking my life over, evaluating what steps I needed to take to be successful, and saying to myself but aloud, "I've got to do this."

It was daunting. It was a challenge. I took hold of my courage, pulled myself together, and resigned to make a life for myself as best I could. I had a plan. It was a good plan. I was going to be a sailor again.

Right away I saw that the Washington, D.C. that I had known as a child and into my formative years was gone.

Obstacles stood before me. Day by day I realized the world that I had known had changed. I was struck by just how much changed had taken place.

Becoming familiar with the old neighborhood was refreshing. I remember walking down certain streets and nearly expecting to see the smiling face of a family member or an old friend turn the corner.

But that was not to be. Only the wind whipping at my own face. I remember feeling the loss of so much, the loss of so many family and friends. I remembered the good times. Again, and again.

I knocked on doors of old friends, hoping to be reunited with an old friend, maybe the benefit of a "Welcome home, Greg!" would help me set aside some of the conflicting feelings of ambivalence that I had. But life had changed dramatically. Some of the doors were not even standing.

One afternoon I went to the family home of two old friends, brothers Don and Steven. These two brothers had been good friends of mine when I was a teenager. Together, they had been a positive influence.

Don and Steven had lost their mom some years before, and they now shared the family home (with another sibling); electing to keep the property and live there. We chatted and caught up on the decades that had passed.

On more than a few occasions that had encouraged me to choose a path other than that of a rogue and vagabond. Don had been in the Navy, and he always imparted a sea story or two upon me.

I rang the doorbell. It had been such a long time, I expected their mother or other family member to answer, maybe tell me where my friends were now living.

I was surprised when both Don and Steven came to the door. Seeing me, recognizing me immediately, Don swung open the door and exclaimed with astonishment, "Greg White! Greg White!" Don and Steve examined me quickly, with energetic surprise. Their combined surprise was remarkable.

Don said, "Greg, we thought somebody had killed you a long time ago!"

Don's words were sobering. Words of alarm, yet in a subtle way. His words could have very well been true. It was a reality that the life I had known on the street as a young person had been reckless and full of real danger.

And "yes" there had been more than a handful of harrowing moments, close calls. I had been in dozens of fights. Cut, stabbed, and shot with a stray bullet. The isolation of solitary confinement and other strict punishments had been no fairy tale world. Just to emerge with my sanity was an achievement.

I had been incarcerated during the entire "crack cocaine epidemic" that had destroyed many areas of Washington, D.C. When the city was "under siege" I was a thousand miles away under wraps in solitary-confinement.

I had effectively been removed from the stage and scene of a bad time in our society when life and death was exchanged on city streets for a cheap price – sometimes as cheap as the price of a ten dollar bag of illicit narcotics.

Having ran with a rough crowd of young people presented food for thought [for myself]. The areas of Washington, D.C. that I knew as a street kid were, by any estimation, dangerous places to be.

Questions formed inside my head: What forces had sent me to prison? What if I were not incarcerated? Would I have experimented with cocaine? Would I have carried a firearm? Would I have fallen victim of my own irresponsibility? But why should I, or anyone, have to suffer the discord of being in prison for decades to survive the danger involved with being young person?

More than a few of my friends and classmates had not survived the test of time. Some had not reached age thirty before their demise.

Gone were many of the faces that held a sign of friendly trust. Bonds we formed were not without virtue. We had all been looking for something, reaching outward for the promise of a better tomorrow. We had been so young and so full of life. But those lives were gone now. They would not be coming back.

Randy Barnard had been the first young friend lost to the street life. Some of these friends were very close to me. Some are family members.

No matter the impetuous circumstance nor enigmatic event, each loss held a story, each story was unique, and with these stories live memories that have a special place in my heart. The benevolent smile that I saw upon each young face is hard to forget.

Michael "Juggy" Broome
Ronnie Jackson
Clayton Robinson
Edward "Steady Eddie" Harris
Stephanie Williams
Theresa Claiborne
Ivan Spriggs
Clifton "Tank" Spriggs
James "Bronco" McMillan
Anthony "Boo Nog" Staton-Bey
Marlon Haight
Jeffrey Kearns
Andre Pixley
Dawn Wallace
Melvin Williams
Gerald Darlington

Keith "Keithy" Proctor
Nadine "Cuda" Jenkins
Michael Washington
Big Marvin
Oggie Watson
Melvin Watson
Anthony Moore
Ronald Wilkerson
Sharon Cunningham
Anthony "Chuck" Cauley
Timothy "Jay" White
Deborah Archie Smith
Jeannette Murray Smith
Nathaniel "Beaver" Cauley

CHAPTER NINETEEN

Obeying the law was paramount.

Don gave me an older, second-hand bicycle, and it proved to be a great form of inner city transportation. The bicycle used in conjunction with the Metro Bus and Metro Rail (subway) service allowed me to make my way around D.C. and sometimes into the immediate suburban sprawl of the city.

I went to work.

In the beginning, amid the laughter of those within earshot, naysayers who viewed my efforts to turn my life around as being "a waste of time," I found jobs with the temporary employment agency Food Team Inc. "Kitchen Utility" was my job title; duties included washing dishes, pots and pans, taking out garbage, and swabbing decks. I earned $6.25 an hour.

I rode the old bicycle, pinched pennies, and kept my nose to the grind. The excitement of being free was mind-boggling.

Receiving my first paycheck for a thirty-hour week of work I earned $146.75. I thought I was rich!

Sharing my aspiration to become a sailor again was not always met with support. Among the naysayers was a handful of family members. They scoffed and laughed at me. They were critical of me for riding an old bicycle, being a dishwasher, and nearly living in a flophouse. It was painful. And it was a great letdown.

When I spoke of my plans with them, they said, "Impossible!" and offered more statements that were hurtful. It was as though they were in expectation for me to fail.

Some of them agreed, and with an angry attitude, that I was "crazy" to believe that I could change my life.

In this "attitude" I remembered the psychological trauma of being denied, being outcast, and being turned away as a child and teenager.

This was the same lack of encouragement and support that I had known as a young person – from some of these same family members.

What made matters worse was these family members passed the negative opinion and dissension on to others, their children, and their in-law's.

I had not known these children and in-law's due to my separation from society. Some of them had been born while I was far away. But it seems that they were taught a "system" of belief that I was a character not worthy of human want or need. This is a sad commentary – yet one that needs to be shared.

Yet, none of this "attitude" was unique to my own family. I have known other families that were notorious for belittling each other, whether with slight insults, or outright fits of dislike for each other.

But I had to look beyond this circumstance. The energy I exerted when in this company [of people] was exhausting.

I rationalized, 'Why should I subject myself to these negative voices?' More and more I stayed away from those who put me down. In time, I would stay away more and more.

I worked all the overtime hours that I was offered or could volunteer for. I worked 50 to 70 hours per week as a dishwasher. And I kept riding that old bicycle.
Being institutionalized was something that I struggled with. Harboring a head full of "prison thoughts" is what the negative side effects of being institutionalized is all about.

This was another form of trauma from my past, and more recent at that. The measure of this trauma can be gauged best on an individual by individual comparison or inquiry. For comfort, I pushed forward with my work and my ambition.

It was tough at first. But I was determined to re-invent myself. This meant shaking off the attitude, discarding the concepts of projecting an image of a tough guy.

I had to learn not to ball my fists up when I went into a room full of people. I had to control my eyes from searching out what could be used as a makeshift weapon – right away – if something should "jump off" like a disturbance. Pushing thoughts such as these from my mind was a concentrated effort; and I willed myself not to "size up" strangers (in anticipation of a confrontation).

Re-inventing myself started within. It was more than working and obeying the law. I had to re-invent my patterns of thought. I had to remind myself that my spirit was free – just as much so as my physical form.

Grandma was there. Giving me shelter and warmth. Allowing me to pay small amounts of rent money (when I could). Grandma was the Angel that held us all together. She was something very special.

My aunt's Francine, Deborah, and Pearleen were profoundly supportive of my newfound attitude. Younger cousins Anthony and Joey, who were grown now, took me under their wing. Joey gave me bags full of clothing, some of this stuff was new with tags still on, most of it lightly used and in good fit.

For several months, every single day, Anthony would pick me up and we would go out to restaurants and events and social gatherings. Anthony was instrumental in my re-entry into society. He even allowed me to vent my frustrations.

I remember losing my patience with him once, and asking him in a harsh voice, "Do you know who I am? Do you know you are messing with?"

Anthony dead panned, "Uh, you're, Greg. My cousin. Clift's son." I just looked him with a hard look.

And then I softened as his words hit home with the hard impact of truth. Anthony, more than he may know, more than he will probably credit himself, helped me shake off the foolish remnants of being "institutionalize" and conditioned to codes of reason that were non-existent in a free society. I thought back to what Abdullah had said about a "reputation" having no significance.

I found other temporary employment agencies; "Command Labor" and "Ace Temporaries."

These jobs were construction site laborer and clean-up. I accepted all the menial labor jobs I could find.

I relished manual labor with wheel barrows, hauling construction site debris and trash. With boots on I went into ditches with a shovel and made holes and trenches.

Not for a second did I complain. I knew that my life was my own responsibility, and that if I wanted to progress in life that I would have to make substantial sacrifices. I understood well that I had created my circumstances, and that the energy to change my circumstances would some from myself.

Saving money, $25 or $30 at a time, I purchased an old car, a 1990 Honda and paid $240 in cash for the title. And then I had to teach myself how to drive; accomplishing this by driving along side streets, quiet streets, late at night when there was very little traffic and small chance of having an accident.

The more I drove into the night, the better driver I became. I failed the practical driving examination twice before passing on my third effort.

When I drove my old car, a "box Honda" they called it, more snickers and laughter came from some of those around me; some were family members, some were co-workers, and some were people that I had known from the street life and in jail. Really, I was chided and held in contempt for embarking on a genuine effort to move forward in my life.

Belittled, derided, I ignored the laughter and I went back to work: washing dishes, ditch-digging, washing pots & pans, hauling lumber, hawking newspapers, painting, cutting grass, working in a laundry, odd jobs, concierge jobs, temporary office jobs. And driving that old "box Honda" around.

I had to make my way in the world. I had to stay grounded and focused on my goal to become a sailor. And so, I worked hard. Sometimes I worked eighty hours a week.

Laughter continued when I said, "I'm going to be a sailor again."

Bad dreams and unpleasant memories have haunted me. Putting negatives to rest has been the struggle of my life. But I was going to be a sailor again, and nothing could deter me from that goal. Knowing that I held some responsibility was sobering.

The desire to become a sailor again burned inside of me – but I would have to bid time on parole for three years before I could submit an application to the United States Coast Guard for a U.S. Merchant Mariners Document, commonly known as a "credential" or a "z-card."

Bruce Clark and I were re-united. Bruce would drive down from New York to D.C. and we would socialize and dine and share ideas for the future. Bruce thought my plan for becoming a sailor again was an excellent choice. What better way to change the course of my life?

Continuing with hard work, I saved money and traveled by bus or car to New York from time to time. Bruce and I had the run of Manhattan, and it seemed like old times in a lot of ways.

Life was not without struggle. But I had been toiling for the balance of my life. I worked long hours. I earned little income. But I was content. Set free of prison had a profound effect on me. The freedom was almost unreal. The choices before me were phenomenal.

With a resolve that was fixed and unwavering, I slept with positive thoughts and ideas on my side, knowing that one day, and soon, my life would change for the better. I pushed forward, making amends.

With the successful completion of my parole terms, my sentence and penalties met, my debt was paid.

Drafting a formal petition, I requested official adjudication. My request was granted, and with an executive letter and order, I received, through this adjudication, final closure for each one of my violations of the law.

My civil rights were fully restored.

CHAPTER TWENTY

And then it happened!

In September 2007, Captain Pete Bolster, Jeff's brother, offered me my first job as a professional mariner; the position being Mate/Educator aboard the small vessel M/V Mildred Belle for the Living Classrooms Foundation Shipboard Department in Baltimore. This was the "green light" that I had searched for with diligence, commitment, and tenacious resolve.

More opportunity came. With an "Entry Level" Merchant Mariners Document I toiled and made step by step effort as a documented sailor.

Through union halls, maritime recruiters, and "head hunters" I have found jobs on a dozen or more deep sea going ships in the Atlantic, the Pacific, and the Indian Ocean, the Caribbean Sea, The Gulf of Mexico, the South China Sea, the Bay of Bengal, and on the Great Lakes. All over the world to be sure.

Accruing the required sea service, I submitted the required applications to the U.S. Coast Regional Examination Centers to be processed at the National Maritime Center.

With sea service, professional training, and hands-on experience I successfully passed each exam mandated to earn my [first] rating as a Qualified Member of the Engine Department (QMED) Oiler. This endorsement allowed me to pursue watch-standing Engineering Department jobs.

Saving what money I could, at times borrowing money from family and friends, I was fortunate to attend the "Maritime Institute of Technology & Graduate Studies" (MITAGS) in Lithicum, Maryland. There, I was able to earn my initial STCW-95 endorsement of Basic Safety Training.

"Tall Ships America" in Newport, Rhode Island awarded me an educational grant to help with tuition fees.

With that grant I enrolled at the "Mid-Atlantic Maritime Academy" in Norfolk, Virginia, and earned additional STCW-95 endorsements (Rating Forming Part of an Engineering Watch, Advanced Firefighting, Proficiency in Survival Craft-Lifeboatman, Medical Care Provider, and First Aid/CPR/AED. The training and exams were beneficial.

When not taking classes I was going to sea, working and earning "sea service" which was the method of merit to qualify a seaman for upgrades. And I when I had saved enough money, earned enough sea service, I enrolled in U.S. Coast Guard approved licensed marine diesel engineer course at Mid-Atlantic Maritime. I completed the course. All exam modules were passed.

On 10 June 2015 I was issued a U.S. Coast Guard Merchant Mariners Officer's License as a Chief Engineer OSV and Designated Duty Engineer 1000-4000hp. For me, this was a milestone. The long way home to be sure.

Now, I was a merchant marine officer.

Jeff Bolster and Ken Ringle have become good friends of mine. We have met and had lunch or dinner on several occasions; and we communicate regularly by telephone and email.

Jeff and I have shared more than a few stages together, speaking engagements, and being present for the screening of a short documentary film that was produced by the National Endowment for the Humanities (NEH).

The short film is entitled "The Scholar and the Sailor" and can be found on the NEH website, as well as on Meridian Hill Pictures website and on "YouTube."

Receiving a letter from a school teacher, Susan Hammond, was a surprise for me. Her 6th grade class of students at the Crossroads School in Baltimore had learned of my story (published in the Washington Post in May 2012) and decided to write letters to me as part of learning assignment – I received dozens of letters from these students.

Since then, I have traveled to Baltimore and met with inner city students at the Crossroads School on two occasions.

In Norfolk, I met with Captain Daniel Moreland of the Barque Picton-Castle. Bruce and I traveled to Virginia together to meet within the Captain and spend time on the Picton-Castle.

I met with Captain Michael Schneider, USN Retired, of PROJECT LIBERTY SHIP in Baltimore, one of the seaman that I corresponded with from prison, and we discussed how my career as a merchant mariner had taken shape and became a reality.

With the advancement of "social media" and other contemporary forms of communication, I was graced to re-connect with a number of my old shipmates - the sailors - the plank owners - and my friends that I knew from 16 December 1978 aboard the USS Moosbrugger DD-980.

I found Mike Warren, Dutch Schroeder, Bob Seckinger, Brian Hulse, Tom Totoris, Mike Morris, Denis Taylor, Rick Linares, Don Brown, Sam Vidal, Greg Nash, Armando Mendoza, Randy Klump, and Randy Gordon's wife (Melanie "Still Standing" Gordon).

In Seattle, coming off a ship, I connected with Mike Warren again. We left boot camp in 1978 and were Plank Owners on the 'Moose.

Over a five year span of time, whenever in Seattle, Mike and I would get together. Always breakfast, lunch, or dinner. Mike had retired from the Navy with the rank of Chief Petty Officer, and he applauded me for turning my life around.

I remember him saying, "I always wondered what happened to you, Greg." Sadly, Mike passed away in 2016. His passing was a great loss. We were shipmates and friends.

Petty Officer 2nd Class Bernard Van Meter, Plank owner, Oil King, and my first supervisor aboard the 'Moose, and I would chat over the telephone. I told him my goal to become a sailor again. He was amazed, encouraged me without a second guess. More sadness, he passed away before I earned my first U.S. Merchant Mariners Credential.

Remarkably, I found my old partner Earl Bennett. He was astonished to receive a letter from me.

Days later he wrote back saying, "I never forgot you, Greg. I swear I was just telling a [friend] about you yesterday! and today I get a letter from you! This is unbelievable. How did you find me? How did you find me like this?"

Through the strength of friendship, Bruce Clark and Rick Linares and I were fortunate enough to stay connected without any great lapse of time throughout the past four (4) decades. Forty long years.

On short notice, in late 2013, I made a "pier head jump" and took a shipping contract aboard an oceanographic research vessel (owned by the Office of Naval Research or ONR).

This employment contract, commonly referred to as "a ticket," would take me, by air and sea, from Washington, D.C. to Hong Kong, China, to Kaohsiung, Taiwan, to Colombo, Sri Lanka, to Paris, France (for a three day layover), to New York, New York, and back to Washington, D.C. It was a ticket around the world; a legitimate circumnavigation of the planet Earth by air and sea.

Traveling 'round the world had been a childhood dream. The games we played on "Pirate Lake" had a phenomenal effect on me, one that has stood the test of time. Just getting out of Washington, D.C. in 1978 for the very first time was an accomplishment. But the three days I spent in Paris were outstanding!

Redeeming myself, earning a U.S. Coast Guard license as a Chief Engineer OSV and Designated Duty Engineer 4000 HP has been a fulfillment. Being a sailor has been the central passion of my life. It is the one goal that has governed my imagination and reality.

"I'm going."

AFTERWORD

The 40th Anniversary/Reunion of the USS Moosbruger was held over the 2018 Memorial Day weekend in North Charleston, South Carolina. I was able to be there.

It was a great event. Well organized and scheduled by fellow 'Moose sailors who had also served aboard her. Namely Chuck Cribbs and Pete Murray. All of us had stood the test of time. The choices that we made, good or bad or half-ass, have been choices that we have had to live with. I am elated to see how we all have kept the 'Moose close to heart.

Four decades of "hell and high water" has passed for each one of the Plank Owners who were able to attend. I was overwhelmed to reunite with Matthew "Dutch" Schroeder, Mike Morris, Brian Hulse, Tom Totoris, Denis Taylor, Jimmy Campbell, Mike Guiry, Phil Dunn, and Bill Jones.

Bruce Clark and Rick Linares, although unable to attend the reunion, have been with me through thick and thin. Day by day, Bruce has been within my reach over the course of the past forty years: 1978 – 2018.

Rest in peace to the Plank Owners: Mike Warren, Bernard Van Meter, Jeffrey Depas, Wayne "Preacher" Jones, Ricky Kloepper, Brodick, and Boone.

With appreciation I remember each of the Plank Owners who came to my rescue; especially the shipmates in "Snipes Castle" no matter the rhyme or reason, thank you all. Being a sailor was something special. Being an engineer was the best.

"Once a snipe, always a snipe."

RETROSPECT

There we were, my father and I, on a cold and blustery Christmas Morning in 1966, out on the open asphalt of a large parking lot. I was six-years old, and my dad had presented me with a spectacular gift. It was a brand new, gold painted Huffy Penguin bicycle with 20-inch wheels, Hi-Rise handle bars, and a genuine faux leopard print banana style seat. All the kids my age wanted such a bicycle. I beamed with joy.

Time with my father, Frank Clifton, was always full of excitement and expectation. My parents were young, and while they no longer remained joined as a couple, my dad never missed a birthday or holiday or even an ordinary weekend. Unbeknownst to me, he made remarkable effort to be an active part of my childhood. He was always there. Concerned. Constant. Consistent.

The wind blew strong and cold, sweeping hard and stiff against our faces. We had a tough time trying to attach the training wheels to the bicycle. Finally, or so we reasoned, we were all set and ready for me to ride.

Clumsily, but with purpose, I mounted the Huffy, fitting onto the seat, and focused on taking my first two-Wheel ride. My dad guided, supported and coached me.

The training wheels buckled and twisted. They were a hindrance, not a help, and, after some long minutes, my dad declared, "Forget the training wheels! You can ride this, dude. I know you can ride it."

With that confident resolve, he removed the training wheels, tossed them aside, and said, "Saddle up, dude, you can do it."

He held the Huffy steady and sure (by the tail of the banana seat) and, walking behind the bicycle, he encouraged me with "Pedal, Gregory, pedal," and I complied.

We picked up momentum. He trotted slowly behind the bicycle as I pedaled. The balance came naturally. The balance was sure. The wind was pushing me from behind.

"Keep pedaling! You can do it! You can do it, dude!" my dad encouraged with vigor as we picked up speed and the bicycle, seemingly, came alive with magic and motion. I sensed power in my effort. I felt power in my pedal. It was exciting. It was fantastic.

My father was animated as he urgently coached me to victory, "Go! Go! Look at him go!" he shouted as he released his hold on the bicycle seat, "Look at him go! Look at him go!"

And I was gone. Riding with the wind.

Pumping and turning the wheels, finding balance with motion, streaking brazen and gutsy across the cold and vacant parking lot, I rode my first "big boy" bike and gained the confidence to take that next step into another stage of my childhood.

There would be other moments with dad that shaped themselves into keepsakes: My first pair of Chuck Taylor's, when I was 12 years old. First skateboard, first kite, first 5-speed bicycle, first double cheeseburger at Jr. Hot Shoppes, first pair of Lee Jeans, first Kung Fu movie at The Town Theater on New York Avenue N.W., first advice on girls and dating. We had grown closer with each and every turn that life held for us.

Decades later, as Thanksgiving Day was approaching, I decided to spend the holiday with my father. He had been ill, and he was resigned to remain rooted to his sofa, perched before the 40 inch flat-screen television that he loved to watch.

I decided that I would cook my first Thanksgiving dinner and take the food over to my dad's apartment and eat with him. There had been a number of major holidays that I had not shared with my father. I had left home at 17 to join the men (and women) who down to the sea in ships. I became a sailor.

Life had taken fantastic turns for both of us. There had been ups and downs and a grave measure of trial and circumstance. The story of my struggles have been noted and documented. Taking responsibility for my mistakes and errors was a key factor in making the balance of my life stable and without shame.

In spirit and endeavor, I remained a sailor. And as a professional seaman I'm away nearly all the time. To mark my travels, my dad had purchased a globe of the world, and he kept it close at hand on an end table in his living room.

With the help and guidance of a dear friend, Sharon, I gathered all the necessary ingredients, all the seasoning and spices, all the trimmings, and we rinsed and washed and cooked and roasted.

As the food for the meal began to come together, I thought about some of the past meals that my dad had prepared for me when I was a child. I thought the thick and greasy grilled cheese sandwiches that he taught me how to make, and I remembered the cups of milk that he poured, how he was careful not to fill the cup too close to the brim, taking caution not to spill, while prodding me in a cheery tone, "Drink up, chum, and you'll be strong and wise!"

Finally, Sharon and I loaded the meal into her car, and then we made off, driving across the city to my father's apartment.

Thanksgiving Day dinner went very well. My father had never been much of a grand eater, unlike myself, and he ate sparingly but with interest and enjoyment.

It was a good meal. My father, Sharon and I were happy to be together. We had much to be thankful for.

Two days later, I had my sea bag stuffed and packed with sailor's gear, and I was flying off to Seattle, Washington, to join a research ship and then sail the open sea north and into Ketchikan, Alaska.

While dockside in the shipyard in Seattle, as was my habit, I telephoned my father every day to see how he was doing. November went, December came, and then it was January 1st, 2013. New Year's Day!

"Happy New Year, dude!" my father greeted me as we chatted over the telephone. I was excited about the possibilities of a new year. My dad had been ill, but his spirit had been strong, and his sensibilities remained wise.

For the most part of the year I would be at sea in Alaskan waters, venturing into the Bering Sea, and sharing the adventure of a lifetime; and when I returned home I would bring trinkets and sea tales of romantic guise. The new year would be full of excitement.

In the early morning hours of 3 January 2013, my father passed away on the sofa in his home. After speaking with my dad on New Year's Day I would not hear his voice again. My mother, whose given name was Mary Elizabeth, had passed away nine-years earlier.

I was now without my parents; two kids who had taken on the unwitting responsibility of raising me in a haphazard, hit and miss, manner. I have no doubt, they did the best they could do.

But the memories remain strong. The stories passed down to me are with merit. Walking past what was The Tivoli Theater at 14th Street & Park Road N.W., the spot where my parents dated for the very first time, I can close my eyes and picture my father's distinctive gait as I imagine the two of them walking hand in hand.

In my reverie I can imagine the emboldened theater marquee lights advertising the main feature being shown, which was, "The Creature From the Black Lagoon."

Later, and even after they grew apart and were no longer a couple, my mother would periodically remind me with poised demeanor and strength, "Your father was always good to everyone."

She would look me in the eye, adding, "When I first met your father I didn't know what love was. I was only thirteen years old. I was too young to know what love was. I just liked him. He dressed real nice. He was smart and cute. But we were too young to know what love was.

After you were born, and after he did everything he could to take care of you, I respected him a lot, and eventually I came to love him. And I did. I loved Clift. I loved the ground that he walked on."

My father frequently encouraged me, "Saddle up, dude, you can do it!" He had hoisted me up as a child and carried me whenever I grew tired when we out in the city. I thought of this while carrying a small box containing his cremains, cradled close in my arms, as I entered the lobby area of the apartment house where I live.

I was bringing my dad home with me. Each step I took was careful and sure. Careful not to falter. Careful not to lose my balance. The small box in hand nearly crushed my heart.
In the coming seasons, I plan to put forth one last Father's Day gesture. With a ship's Captain's nod and grace, I hope to bring my father's cremains out to sea with me.

There will be a scripture reading. There will be a silent reflection. With love and respect, I shall release my father's ashes into the wind to be spread far and wide across the deep blue sea.

Remembering his own words, I will whisper, "Look at him go, look at him go."

U.S. MERCHANT MARINER DOCUMENTATION

U.S. Coast Guard Merchant Mariner Credential (MMC) and STCW-95 Endorsements,

III/1: Officer In Charge of an Engineering Watch In a Manned Engine-Room or DDE in a Periodically Unmanned Engine Room (OICEW)
III/3: Chief Engineer & 2ND Engineer Officers (1 AE) Between 1,000 Hp and 4,000 Hp (3000Kw)
III/4: Rating forming part of a watch in a manned engine room or designated to perform duties in a periodically unmanned engine room (RFPEW)
III/5: Able Seafarer-Engine
VI/1: Basic Training (BT)
VI/2: Proficiency in the use of survival craft, rescue boats and fast rescue boats
VI/3: Advanced Fire Fighting
VI/4 First Aid and Medical Care Provider
VI/6 Vessel Personnel with Designated Security Duties, Security Awareness
Designated Duty Engineer 1000/4000 HP (3000Kw)
Qualified Member of the Engine Department (QMED)- ANY RATING, Ratings Being:
• OILER
• JUNIOR ENGINEER
• PUMPMAN/MACHINIST
• FIREMAN/WATERTENDER
• ELECTRICIAN/REFRIGERATION ENGINEER

Vanuatu License Chief Engineer
Commonwealth of the Bahamas Seaman's Record Book
Tropical Helicopter Underwater Escape Training (T-HUET) with Sea Survival Exercises
SAFE GULF Training
Transportation Workers Identification Credential (TWIC)

SHIPBOARD EXPERIENCE

July 2018 – Intermittent, Chief Engineer, R/V Atlantic Explorer, National Science Foundation, Bermuda Institute of Ocean Sciences, St. Georges, Bermuda

February 2018 – Intermittent, 2nd Assistant Engineer, R/V Oceanus, National Science Foundation, Oregon State University, Newport, Oregon

August 2017 – October 2017, QMED-ANY RATING, Ship's Security Officer, Maine Maritime Academy, Training Ship State of Maine (TSSOM), Castine, Maine

May 2017 – July 2017, Chief Engineer, M/V J.S. Stone, Carmuese Lime & Stone, Great Lakes, Erie, Pennsylvania

September 2016 – March 2017, Chief Engineer, T/B Arthur Foss, FOSS MARITIME COMPANY, Port of Long Beach, California

March 2016 – April 2016, QMED-OILER, M/V Ocean Grand (Tramp Bulk Carrier), Crowley Maritime Corporation – Caribbean Sea, New Orleans, Louisiana

September 2015 – October 2015, QMED-OILER on DSV Midnight Star, Maritime Management Services, Gulf of Mexico, Port Fourchon, Louisiana

June 2015 – August 2015, 1st Assistant Engineer (limited), R/V Oceanus (National Science Foundation) – Pacific Ocean. Oregon State University, Newport, Oregon

February 2015 - April 2015, QMED-Oiler, USNS Narragansett T-ATF-167 (Military Sealift Command), Fleet Tug - Pacific Ocean, Caribbean Sea, Gulf of Mexico, Atlantic Ocean. Don Jon Marine, Inc., San Francisco, California

December 2014 - January 2015, QMED-Oiler on R/V Thomas G. Thompson (Office of Naval Research) - Gulf of Alaska (Pacific Ocean), University of Washington School of Oceanography, Seattle, Washington

November 2014 - December 2014, Motorman (QMED-Oiler) on Pacific Sharav, Drillship (DP-6 Vessel) - Gulf of Mexico, Pacific Drilling Co., Port Fourchon, Louisiana

March 2014 - April 2014, QMED-Oiler on MSV Global Orion (DP-2 Vessel, Dive Support, Seismic Research) - Gulf of Mexico, TechNip, Carlyss, Louisiana

October 2013 - December 2013, QMED-Oiler, R/V Roger Revelle (Office of Naval Research) - Indian Ocean, South China Sea, Pacific Ocean, Scripps Institution of Oceanography, San Diego, California

May 2013 - July 2013, QMED-Oiler, R/V Ocean Starr (DP-2 Vessel, NOAA Fisheries Contract) Pacific Ocean, U.S. Department of Commerce, Seattle, Washington

November 2012 - March 2013, QMED-Oiler, NOAA Ship Fairweather, Oceanographic Survey Ship, Pacific Ocean, Puget Sound, Gulf of Alaska, U.S. Department of Commerce, Seattle, Washington, Ketchikan, Alaska

July 2012 - October 2012, QMED-Oiler, R/V Ocean Pioneer (DP-1 Vessel, Seismic Research) Pacific Ocean, Stabbert Maritime & Ocean Services, Port Hueneme, California

April 2012, Unlicensed Engineer, L/B Bourg (Lift Boat) – Gulf of Mexico, Offshore Marine, Venice, Louisiana

September 2011 – January 2012, OS & Oiler on R/V Ocean Carrier (DP-2 Vessel, Dive Support, Seismic Research) – Gulf of Mexico, Stabbert Maritime & Ocean Services, Port Fourchon, Louisiana

February 2008 – December 2008, THE POTOMAC RIVERBOAT COMPANY, Alexandria, Virginia

September 2007 – November 2007, Mate/Educator, M/V Mildred Belle, S/V Lady Maryland, Baltimore Harbor, Chesapeake Bay, The Living Classrooms Foundation- Shipboard Department, Baltimore, Maryland

November 1978 – October 1980, USS Moosbrugger DD-980, United States Navy, Charleston, South Carolina

SPEAKING PRESENTATIONS

13 July 2012, National Endowment for the Humanities (Council Meeting), Washington, D.C.

13 September 2012, The Crossroads School (Community Meeting), Baltimore, Maryland

05 February 2013, Boston University (Presentation), Boston, Massachusetts

03 March 2013, The Crossroads School (Community Meeting), Baltimore. Maryland

13 February 2014, District of Columbia Council for the Humanities and NEH Film Screening

15 May 2014, The Crossroads School, Baltimore, Maryland

The Washington Post newspaper published an article on May 19, 2012, written by Gregory White regarding the subject matter of this book.

Meridian Hill Pictures of Washington, D.C. produced an award winning short film, "The Scholar & The Sailor," funded by the National Endowment for the Humanities – detailing the connection and friendship between Gregory White and Professor W. Jeffrey Bolster from the University of New Hampshire, and the author of the book "BLACK JACKS: African American Seamen in the Age of Sail," (Harvard University Press 1997).

"The Scholar & The Sailor" was awarded the WHEATON FILM FESTIVAL 2017 Levin Grand Prize for Best Film. The film can be viewed online at:

https://www.neh.gov/films/the-scholar-and-the-sailor

And on YouTube

Thank you all for your caring, patience, and support:

My wife, Blanca (the peach of my life). My parents, my grandparents, my siblings, my aunts and uncles, my cousins, especially aunt's Francine, Deb, and Pearleen, and cousins Najiy Hassan Shabazz and Anthony, and Joey.

Jeff Bolster, Pete Bolster, Dan Moreland, Biff Bowker, Ken Ringle, Sandra Wilkinson, Susan Hammond, Lance Kramer, Ellie Walton, Brandon Kramer, Meridian Hill Pictures, Wheaton Film Festival, John W. Davis III, Ray Moody, Mike Schneider, Judy Havemann, Lynn Medford, Muwakkil aka Teddy, Deb Heard, Wil Haygood, Eric Penn, Martin Desmond, Bronco, Troop, Kemp-El, Dale Boyd, Mark Bradley, Dave Bean, Big George, and our entire generation of all those who have painstakingly redeemed themselves, and in memory of those who we have lost.

Author Contact:

Gregory White
northsidereport@aim.com

Made in the USA
Middletown, DE
26 February 2023

25213791R00139